Washington Historic Places

ON THE NATIONAL REGISTER

Richard Moreno

Washington Historic Places

On the National Register

Richard Moreno

2026
Mountain Press Publishing Company
Missoula, Montana

Library of Congress Cataloging-in-Publication

Names: Moreno, Richard author
Title: Washington historic places on the National Register / Richard Moreno.
Description: Missoula, Montana : Mountain Press Publishing Company, 2026. | Includes bibliographical references and index.
Identifiers: LCCN 2026001392 | ISBN 9780878427246 paperback
Subjects: LCSH: Historic sites—Washington (State) | Monuments—Washington (State) | Washington (State) | National Register of Historic Places | LCGFT: Guidebooks
Classification: LCC F892 .M667 2026 | DDC 917.9704—dc23/eng/20260212
LC record available at https://lccn.loc.gov/2026001392

PRINTED IN THE USA BY VERSA PRESS, INC.

Mountain Press
PUBLISHING COMPANY
P.O. Box 2399 • Missoula, MT 59806 • 406-728-1900
800-234-5308 • info@mtnpress.com
www.mountain-press.com

PREFACE AND ACKNOWLEDGMENT

While every book project requires the help and assistance of many people, this one could not have been completed without the aid of my wife, Pam, who supported me and, most importantly, served as my driver during many parts of my journey to visit each of the places mentioned here. In addition to serving as my companion and sounding board during our trips, she took the wheel whenever my deathly and irrational fear of high places—particularly when driving on steep cliff roads and over tall bridges—was about to become an impediment. For that, and for so many other things, I thank her, and I dedicate this book to her.

This was not a book I set out to write. When we moved to central Washington a decade ago, we did so because I had accepted a midlevel administrative position with a state university so we could be closer to members of my family, who lived in the Vancouver area. While I love writing, and have been fortunate enough to have had several books published, including *The Roadside History of Nevada* for Mountain Press, the job proved to be fairly consuming with very little time for any personal writing. But I still had the itch.

Fast forward to a few years ago and I retired from that job. Looking around for new writing projects to work on, I reached out to Mountain Press to inquire about writing a *Roadside History of Washington* book since I noticed one had not been published. Former Editor-in-Chief Jennifer Carey, was interested but countered with a different proposal, how would I like to write a Washington Historic Places book? And with that, I was in.

This has been an incredibly fun book to research and write (in spite of any bridges and cliff roads). It has given me an excuse—not that I really needed one—to visit and explore nearly every part of the state, often with my wife and sometimes with my son, Hank. In the process of writing it, I have learned a great deal about the state of Washington and its fascinating history, which I now have an opportunity to share with you. I hope you enjoy reading about these places as much as I enjoyed writing about them.

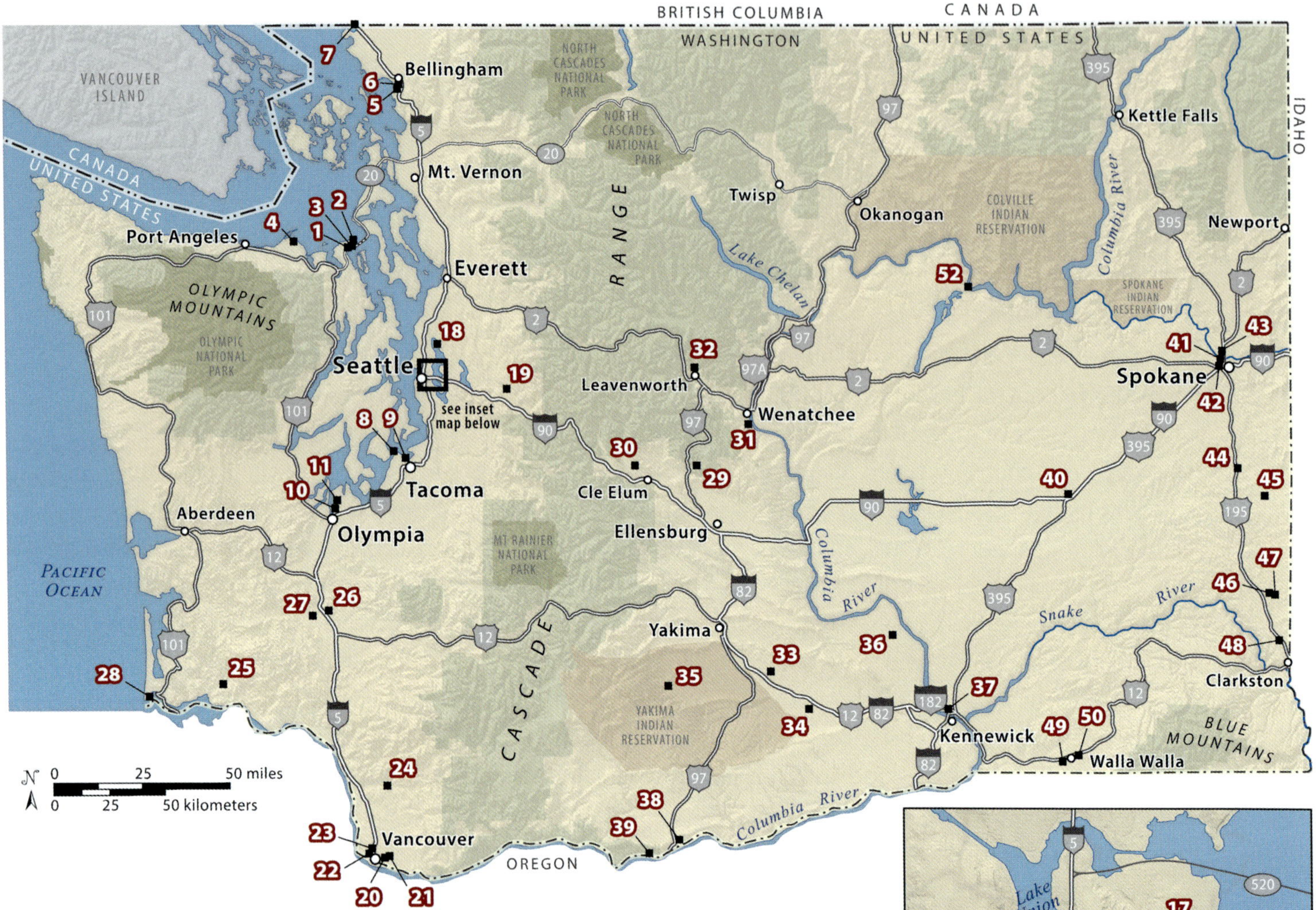

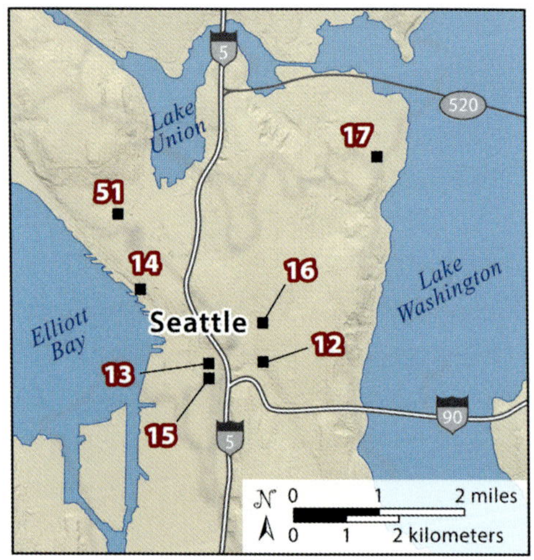

1. Port Townsend Historic District
2. Fort Worden Historical State Park
3. Jefferson County Courthouse
4. Dungeness Schoolhouse
5. Leopold Hotel
6. Whatcom Museum of History and Art
7. Peace Arch
8. Fort Nisqually
9. Stadium High School
10. Washington State Capitol Complex
11. Old State Capitol Building
12. Nihon Go Gakko
13. Chinatown-International District
14. Pike Place Public Market Historic District
15. King Street Station
16. Washington Hall
17. Samuel Hyde House
18. Saint Edwards Seminary
19. Snoqualmie Falls
20. Fort Vancouver Historic Site
21. Washington State School for the Blind
22. House of Providence
23. Covington House
24. Cedar Creek Grist Mill
25. Grays River Covered Bridge
26. St. Helens Hotel
27. Claquato Church
28. Cape Disappointment Historic District
29. Liberty Ghost Town
30. Roslyn Historical Cemeteries
31. Wells House
32. Leavenworth Ski Hill Historic District
33. Teapot Dome Service Station
34. Marble Ranch Round Barn
35. Fort Simcoe Historical State Park
36. Manhattan Project National Historic Park
37. James Moore Mansion
38. Maryhill Museum of Art
39. Wishram Indian Village Site
40. Ritzville Carnegie Library
41. Monroe Street Bridge
42. Patsy Clark Mansion
43. Benewah Milk Bottle
44. Steptoe Battlefield State Park Heritage Site
45. J.C. Barron Flour Mill
46. United Presbyterian Church/Greystone Church
47. Albert W. Thompson Hall
48. St. Boniface Church, Convent, and Rectory
49. Whitman Mission National Historic Site
50. Liberty Theatre
51. The Space Needle
52. Grand Coulee Dam

—Map created by Chelsea M. Feeney, Custom Cartographics (www.cmcfeeney.com)

CONTENTS

The Strait of Juan De Fuca, between the Olympic Peninsula and Vancouver Island, BC.

INTRODUCTION

It's mind-boggling to think that the state of Washington has more than 1,600 places listed on the National Register of Historic Places. All of these places are there because of their proven historical importance, which makes them worthy of being recognized and (I hope) preserved.

The National Register includes everything from historic battlefields to fancy Victorian-era mansions to a dairy retail outlet shaped like a giant milk bottle. Places on the list are found in every one of Washington's 39 counties, with the smallest number (3) found in Garfield County and the largest number (some 310) in King County, Washington's most populous county.

In selecting the places I have featured in this book, I considered factors such as geographic balance, cultural and ethnic significance, and, of course, whether it had a good back story to tell. Naturally, with so many places to choose from, there was also a subjective element in the process—was it a place I wanted to visit and write about?

I've grouped these places into five geographic regions. I did not include any properties that have restrictions on public access, such as private homes, Native American burial sites, or sensitive heritage locations.

Washington is still a relatively young state, having only achieved statehood in November 1889. The first recorded visit by a non-native was in 1774, when Spanish explorer Juan Perez dropped anchor off the Washington coast near present-day Vancouver Island. In the course of his travels along the coast, Perez spotted majestic Mount Olympus in Washington, which he named "Cerro Nevada de Santa Rosalia" or "the Snowy Peak of Saint Rosalia."

The first non-natives to have actually set foot in what is now the state of Washington are believed to have been Spanish explorers Bruno Heceta and Juan Francisco de Bodega y Quadra, who, in 1775, anchored their ships, the *Santiago* and the *Sonora*, at what is now Point Grenville, north of Aberdeen. Heceta led a landing party of twenty-three men ashore and claimed the area for Spain.

Of course, long before then, the place that would become the state of Washington was the home of indigenous peoples, who are believed to have migrated south from Canada and Alaska more than 8,000 years ago. They found rivers filled with fish and abundant forests that provided wood for hunting tools and for building shelters and canoes.

These first people also left their mark—literally—on boulders and rock walls, where they carved and painted symbols and images, which we call petroglyphs, that we're still not sure how to decipher.

At the time the European explorers first arrived, an estimated 500,000 native people lived in the Pacific Northwest (encompassing the modern-day states of Washington, Oregon, and Alaska as well as the Canadian province of British Columbia). Within about a decade, that number was drastically reduced to about 100,000, largely because of the introduction of diseases, particularly smallpox and measles, against which the native people had no immunity. Today, there are twenty-nine federally recognized tribes in the state of Washington.

The sites listed on the National Register are noteworthy because the past often speaks to us through the places and sites that remain. A rectangle of rocks buried in high grass might just be the remains of a 19th-century stone corral, or the foundations of a once-majestic Victorian home, or a prehistoric hunting site. An old two-story brick building, plastered with stucco sometime in the mid-20th century, could have been an early opera house, or a pioneer trading post, or a town's first hotel.

The fun, of course, comes in getting out there and exploring these special places, and in discovering the stories behind them. In that way, you find out that a tiny, off-the-beaten-track roadside church in western Washington is the state's oldest house of worship, or that a bridge in eastern Washington—still in use—was once the largest arched concrete bridge ever constructed in America.

That's not to say all of the places on the National Register always have such obvious historic pedigrees. Some of the places listed could best be described as being eclectic or even eccentric. For example, in the central Washington agricultural town of Zillah, you can find a former gas service station (now a visitors' center) shaped like a giant teapot, and there is that oversized milk bottle building (remarkably, one of a pair in the community) in Spokane.

So, what makes a place eligible for being on the National Register? According to the National Park Service, which oversees the Register, the criteria for inclusion are pretty straightforward. The site must:

- Be at least 50 years old
- Be associated with important historical events or the life of a significant historical person
- Represent some distinctive architectural features of a style, type, period, or method of construction
- Have yielded or may be likely to yield information important in prehistory or history

Additionally, the site must have historic integrity, meaning the property retains some type of physical characteristic that was present during the site's historic period that has not been substantially altered.

The National Register criteria also make eligible some cemeteries, birthplaces, and graves of historically important figures, certain religious properties, reconstructed historic places, and properties moved from their original locations.

Not surprisingly, new entries are made nearly every year to the National Register. In recognition of this fact, I've written about two historic places that, while not yet on the official National Register, are obvious candidates for future inclusion. These are Seattle's iconic Space Needle and the magnificent Grand Coulee Dam, the concrete edifice that continues to power and irrigate much of the state of Washington. These I describe in the Afterword.

Of course, part of the enjoyment in exploring Washington's National Register sites is finding out something new or interesting that helps to explain how the Evergreen State came about. It's visiting a place like the Cape Disappointment Lighthouse near Ilwaco, on the state's southwestern coast, and discovering that not only is it located in a spectacularly beautiful area but it's the oldest lighthouse in the state, erected in 1854. It was built to prevent shipwrecks and to guide ships into the Columbia River from the south. And it's touring the Hanford B Reactor Site near Richland and learning that behind the massive, gleaming wall of now-inert metal fuel tubes lies the heart of the nation's first nuclear reactor. This facility produced the plutonium used during the first detonation of a nuclear weapon (the Trinity Test) in New Mexico in 1945—an event recounted in the 2023 film, "Oppenheimer."

And there are so many more fascinating places and their stories.

So let's go exploring.

Tide pools at Salt Creek Recreation Area near Port Angeles on the Olympic Peninsula

NORTHWEST

This upper west corner of Washington contains some of the most beautiful spots in the state, as well as some of its most historic communities. It includes the coastal areas north of Seattle, the lush Olympic Peninsula (home of the Hoh Rain Forest and Olympic National Park), and some of the state's oldest towns. It's where in 1774 the first non-native people set eyes on the land that would become Washington, and where the first European visitors set foot in 1775.

The first non-indigenous settlement established in what would become Washington was at Neah Bay, on the Olympic Peninsula, in May 1792. Known as Nunez Gaona, the community consisted of about ten small houses. However, after about five months it was abandoned, with the settlers relocating to the town of Nootka in British Columbia, Canada, where there were more economic opportunities.

During the early years of the 19th century, the Spanish, English, and Americans resolved their competing claims on the Oregon-Washington region with several agreements, including: the Treaty of Joint Occupation of Oregon, signed by Great Britain and the United States in 1818; the Transcontinental Treaty of 1819, which called for Spain to relinquish any claims it had on the territory; and, in 1846, the Oregon Treaty, which saw Great Britain cede all of its claims to the area to the U.S.

While the state's first permanent, non-native settlement was Fort Vancouver on the Columbia River (at the southern edge of the state), established in 1825, a few communities nearly as old can be found on the Olympic Peninsula, including the port community of Dungeness (originally called New Dungeness), founded in 1851, and Port Townsend, which was settled in 1852.

Of course, the first human habitation in Washington dates back to a far earlier time. More than 15,000 years ago, prehistoric people are believed to have migrated over a land bridge that connected Asia to North America. Gradually they headed south, becoming the ancestors of the indigenous tribes who currently reside in the state, as well as in the rest of what would become the United States. These native people in the northwest part of the state included the Nooksack, S'Klallam, and Lummi people. Many lived in small villages along the north coast and would move seasonally to take advantage of the natural hunting and gathering resources.

1
Port Townsend Historic District

48.1170° N, 122.7604° W

Area bounded by Blaine, Scott, and Walker Streets in downtown Port Townsend

Located on the northeast edge of the Olympic Peninsula, the town of Port Townsend is famous for its well-preserved Victorian-era homes and buildings. A 200-acre area in the downtown comprises the Port Townsend Historic District.

The community of Port Townsend sits on land that was once the dominion of the S'Klallam tribe, who called it "Kah Tai," meaning "to carry" or "pass through." It's believed the S'Klallam used the area as a wintering ground and, in the warmer months, would travel to other places to hunt, fish, and forage.

The first non-natives arrived in the area in the late 1840s. By that time, the bay surrounding the community had already been named Townshend Bay (in 1792) by British Captain George Vancouver after his friend, the Marquis of Townshend. Most of these early visitors generally were only passing through on trading ships bound for other areas.

The first recorded legal claim on S'Klallam land was filed in August 1850 by Henry C. Wilson, a clerk on one of the trading ships. Wilson did not immediately do anything with his holdings, although he returned later that year to take ownership.

In 1851 Alfred A. Plummer and Charles Bachelder, who had passed by the area as passengers on a trading ship, returned with the intention of settling on the Olympic Peninsula. In April of that year, they arrived at Point Hudson, the easternmost part of the future Port Townsend, and filed a donation claim on land about a mile from Wilson's land. The pair built a two-room, 15-by-30-foot cabin, becoming Port Townsend's first permanent residents (by then the "h" had been dropped in the name).

In October of that year, Plummer and Bachelder were joined by Loren B. Hastings and Francis W. Pettygrove, who were seeking somewhere to put down roots for themselves and their families. The four agreed to form a partnership for the purpose of establishing a town. Hastings and Pettygrove quickly filed claims on land between Plummer and Bachelder's holdings and Wilson's claim, which today would be roughly in the center of downtown Port Townsend.

By all accounts, the S'Klallam people were hospitable to all of the newcomers, only wanting some kind of compensation for their land. According to Washington historian John Caldbick, tribal leaders were given some trade goods and told the U.S. government would eventually pay them for the land.

In 1855 the S'Klallam signed the Treaty of Point No Point, which called for the S'Klallam, as well as the nearby Chimakum and Skokomish tribes, to cede ownership of all their land in return for the establishment of small reservations along Hood Canal, the right to hunt and fish in their traditional lands in perpetuity, and a payment of $60,000 from the U.S. government.

Following the creation of the Washington Territory in 1853, which established Jefferson County (with Port Townsend as the county seat), the community began to grow. By 1860 Port Townsend had a population of 264, which made it the seventh most-populated community in the territory.

Starting in the 1880s, Port Townsend's commercial district began to take shape. Along Water Street, several hotels and saloons, frequented by the increasing number of sailors and travelers, were constructed. Additionally, the announcement of plans for a railroad linking Port Townsend to Olympia sparked a building boom.

The impressive structures built during this time include the three-story Palace Hotel, built by a retired sea captain, Henry L. Tibbits, in 1889; the four-story Mount Baker Block Building, erected in 1890; the four-story James and Hastings Building,

The streets of downtown Port Townsend are lined with historic commercial buildings constructed in the late 19th century, such as the James and Hastings Building (left), erected in 1889 for Francis W. James and Lucinda Hastings. Often described as the most picturesque Victorian structure in the Port Townsend Historic District, the three-story Hastings Building (right) was constructed in 1889.

completed in 1889; and the Hastings Building, also completed in 1889, which was later described as the "most elegant building in the city." Additionally, several fine civic structures were built, including the majestic Jefferson County Courthouse, finished in 1892, the U.S. Post Office and Court and Customs House, completed in 1893.

Unfortunately for Port Townsend, the railroad never fully materialized, although a line was built from the city to Quilcene, Washington. The 33-mile route, however, was never profitable and was abandoned in 1914.

The railroad's failure ended the boom times in Port Townsend, which experienced a rapid loss in population (dropping from a high of 4,500 in the mid-1880s to about 3,500 residents by 1900). The development of the Fort Worden military compound, however, soon provided a small measure of stability to the community in the early 20th century. In the late 1920s, the opening of the nearby Crown Zellerbach Port Townsend Mill brought even more prosperity, although the community continued to see its population fluctuate over the next half century.

In the latter part of the 20th century, Port Townsend's remarkable collection of intact Victorian-era buildings and homes caught the eye of architectural historians, who helped residents and investors see the importance of preserving them. As a result of that effort, the Port Townsend Historic District, which encompasses nearly sixty historic commercial and civic structures, was established and placed on the National Register of Historic Places in 1976.

In recent decades, Port Townsend has become a popular place for retirees and an enormously successful tourist destination. Each year, more than two million visitors come to the community to dine, shop, and experience the town's quaint Victorian-era ambience.

2

Fort Worden Historical State Park

48.1392° N, 122.7694° W

On Battery Way East in Port Townsend

In the 1890s, the United States government decided the strategic Puget Sound Naval Shipyard, along with the cities of Seattle, Tacoma, and Everett, needed protection from any potential sea invasion by a hostile foreign power. Its solution was to build a trio of military facilities near the sound's entrance. The three—Fort Flagler on Marrowstone Island, Fort Casey on Whidbey Island, and Fort Worden on the Olympic Peninsula—would become known as the "Triangle of Fire."

Opened in 1902, Fort Worden was the last of the three to be built. All of the forts were equipped with several batteries of heavy guns. Worden boasted the largest number of artillery pieces (forty-one). None, though, ever fired a shot against a hostile enemy.

Fort Worden, however, was not the first development on that site. When the U.S. government selected the area, a portion of it contained the home of Reverend John Barrow Alexander, who served as rector of the St. Paul's Episcopal Church in Port Townsend from 1882 to 1886. Alexander who was actually a British citizen, later served as Queen Victoria's British Vice Consul in Port Townsend and Tacoma.

In 1883 Alexander purchased a 10-acre parcel near Point Wilson, on which he erected a fine brick residence that included a two-story tower that resembled a castle (or a rook from a chess piece). According to local legend, he intended it to be a summer home for him and his bride-to-be, who was living in Scotland. When he traveled there to marry her, however, it is said he discovered she had already wed another. He returned to Port Townsend and used the structure as a temporary residence.

In 1897 Alexander sold his property, including the home, to the U.S. Army, which incorporated it into its plans for the fort. The tower house, which remains standing and is the oldest building on the fort grounds, was later used for storage and as a residence. In recent years, it has become a popular vacation rental property.

Most of the structures found at Fort Worden were constructed between 1904 and 1905, including the Officers' Quarters, which is a series of two-and-a-half-story houses built to the south of the Parade Grounds, and the Enlisted Men's Barracks, a row of large, white structures erected to the north of the Parade Grounds.

The uniform and well-spaced architecture of the fort's structures was described as "formal, purposeful, and graceful" in the fort's National Register nomination. With their grand columns and rectangular designs, the fort's buildings are considered excellent examples of early 20th- century military construction on the West Coast.

On the high ground to the north of the fort buildings are a dozen concrete gun emplacements, called batteries, on which the fort's cannons were once housed. Each of the batteries was named for an Army officer who had been killed in service or had served with valor in one of the nation's wars. The fort itself was named for John L. Worden, a naval officer who had commanded the legendary ironclad, the "Monitor," in its battle with the Confederate ironclad, the "Merrimac," during the Civil War.

In 1953 the fort was declared surplus by the U.S. Government and sold to the state of Washington. It was initially used as a treatment center for young people before it was acquired by Washington State Parks. Today, the fort is a popular recreational complex that offers miles of beach, hiking trails, picnic facilities, and overnight camping. Tours of selected buildings are also available.

The 434-acre Fort Worden Historic District, which encompasses all of the fort's original buildings (more than fifty structures) as well as the Point Wilson Lighthouse, built in 1914, was added to the National Register of Historic Places in 1974.

This castle-like structure was built in 1883 by John B. Alexander, rector of St. Paul's Episcopal Church in Port Townsend and the original owner of the land on which Fort Worden is located. It is the oldest building on the fort site and now serves as overnight lodgings.

3
Jefferson County Courthouse

48.1121° N, 122.7678° W

On Jefferson Street in Port Townsend

It's nearly impossible to overlook the Jefferson County Courthouse in Port Townsend. Built on a bluff above the town, the three-story courthouse, with its iconic 124-foot tall brick and sandstone clock tower, has long been a beacon not only of justice, but also for incoming ships who could see it from miles away.

Built between 1890 and 1892, the courthouse was designed by Willis A. Ritchie, a famed Seattle architect who also designed the Thurston County Courthouse in Olympia (completed in 1892) and the Spokane County Courthouse (constructed in 1894). Ritchie's design was one of eight originally considered by the Jefferson County Board of County Commissioners. His was selected, according to media accounts of the time, because of his prior experience in designing courthouses.

The 31,390-square-foot Jefferson County Courthouse was constructed in the Romanesque Revival style of architecture popular at the turn of the 20th century for civic buildings. Today, it is the second oldest courthouse in Washington (the Columbia County Courthouse in Dayton, which was completed in 1887, is the oldest).

Materials used in building the courthouse included about 4 million smooth red bricks, manufactured in St. Louis, which were shipped to the site. Additionally, 786 tons of ashlar sandstone were shipped from Alaska and used in the building foundation and trim. Eleven stonecutters and twelve brick masons worked on the project during two years of construction. Total cost of the project was about $125,000 (or more than $4.3 million in today's dollars).

Among the noteworthy elements in the courthouse's original design were geometrically-patterned stone tile floors, highly decorated, hand-carved, solid oak paneling in the third-floor courtroom, and corridor hallways accented with cedar wainscoting. In addition to housing the court offices, the building was also home to all other Jefferson County offices. The county jail, which was in the basement, remained in use until the early 1980s.

The magnificent clock tower was built by the E. Howard Watch & Clock Company of Boston, Massachusetts, with both the bell and clock mechanism made of solid brass. According to historic accounts, the bell was transported overland to Port Townsend, while the clock mechanism was shipped around Cape Horn.

In 1912 the courthouse received electrical power, which allowed for the clock to be illuminated at night. The clock operates much like a cuckoo clock does, with large weights (250-pound boxes of brick and stone) on thick cables slowly dropping from the tower to the basement, then winched by hand back to the top of the tower. An electric winch, added in the mid-20th century, means the process now takes about fifteen minutes and is performed once a week.

While the courthouse remains largely as it was when originally built, it has been renovated and updated over the years. In the 1930s, a central boiler was installed and the courtroom was updated in the 1980s. A new slate and copper roof was placed on the structure in the early 1990s. Additional renovations, such as reconfiguring and modernizing the office spaces, were made to the interior of the building in the first decade of the 21st century. The courthouse was added to the National Register of Historic Places in 1973.

Few courthouses in Washington state are as stately and elegant as the Jefferson County Courthouse in Port Townsend, which stands on a bluff overlooking the community.

4
Dungeness Schoolhouse

48.1427° N, 123.1284° W
On Towne Road, north of Sequim

The northern Olympic Peninsula region, where the communities of Sequim (pronounced "Squim") and Dungeness are located, has long been important to the native Nux s'klallam people (which roughly translates as the "strong people"), who are more commonly known as the S'Klallam tribe. The word Sequim, in fact, means "a place to shoot/hunt" in the S'Klallam language.

The S'Klallam fished and harvested in the fresh and salt waters of the area and, according to historians, practiced controlled burning of the local prairie lands in order to better create a habitat for the growth of berries, other edible plants, and new grasses that would attract the deer and elk they hunted.

It is generally believed that the first non-native to encounter the S'Klallam was a Spanish explorer, Captain Manuel Quimper, who came into contact with the tribe in Dungeness Bay in about 1792. That same year, the famed English explorer, Captain George Vancouver, visited the region, which he named New Dungeness, after a famous headland on the south coast of Kent in England.

The first white settlers arrived in the area about 1851 and established the small community of New Dungeness on the west side of the Dungeness River. Within a short time, these settlers had built a pier on the adjacent tidal flats and, in 1857, erected a small lighthouse near the settlement. According to historical records, in the 1880s the settlement moved to the east side of the Dungeness River and, at the time, became known simply as Dungeness.

In 1892 the settlers, who previously had home-schooled their children or operated makeshift schools in their homes, realized there was a serious need for a formal schoolhouse. This led, in May, to the approval of a bond to pay for the acquisition of land and construction of a school building. By August, a contract for the construction had been issued in the amount of $1,673.

The original two-story, wood-frame, rectangular structure included several classrooms, a second-floor auditorium, and a beautiful belfry atop a gabled roof. It was built on a small plot at the crossroads near the Dungeness River, less than a mile south of the shores of Dungeness Bay. When the 35-by-48-foot school opened in February 1897, it had 73 students between 5 and 20 years old and offered classes from first grade through high school. The academic year was four and a half months long.

The school's sole teacher lived in modest quarters on the second floor of the school. Within a few years, the teaching staff, however, had increased to three. In 1921 the school was enlarged with the addition of a two-story west wing. A few years later, the school's secondary students were assigned to other schools in the area and the school focused on providing elementary education. This was the status quo for the next three decades. However, in 1955 the Dungeness School was forced to close due to declining enrollment and school district consolidation. Local students were assigned to schools in nearby Sequim.

Following the closure, the old schoolhouse was leased to the Dungeness Community Club, which utilized it for many years for events and as a community center. The club purchased the building outright in 1967 and, in subsequent years, conducted a number of fundraising campaigns to maintain and refurbish the building. In 1988 the schoolhouse was added to the National Register of Historic Places.

A few years later, in 1995, the club found itself struggling to keep up with the rapidly increasing costs of preserving and maintaining the building and donated it to the nonprofit Sequim Museum & Arts. The organization operates several local historic properties, including a history museum in Sequim. Today, it rents the facility for special events and offers arts and crafts programs and classes. In 2008 the schoolhouse's belfry, including the original school bell, were restored.

Opened in 1897, the Dungeness Schoolhouse served several generations of local students until it closed in 1955. Since then, it has been used as a community center with local arts and crafts classes.

5
Leopold Hotel

48.4457° N, 122.2843° W

On Cornwall Avenue in downtown Bellingham

Bellingham's Leopold Hotel, now simply known as "The Hotel Leo," is said to have been the first place a person could get a legal alcoholic drink in that city when Prohibition ended in 1933 (allegedly because the alcohol was brought in from nearby Canada, which never prohibited alcohol sales and consumption).

Over the years, the downtown landmark hosted many famous people, such as Clark Gable, who stayed there while filming *The Call of the Wild* in the early 1930s, as well as U.S. President William H. Taft, explorer Richard Byrd, and the controversial evangelist Billy Sunday.

The current Leopold, however, wasn't the first hotel on that site. In 1899 sea captain Josiah B. Byron built a fifty-room hotel on land he owned on Dock Street (now known as Cornell Avenue), which he named the Byron House Hotel.

In addition to owning the hotel, Byron served as a Whatcom town councilman for several years. In that latter role, he was said to have been instrumental in the funding of proper sidewalks and streets in Whatcom. In 1903 Whatcom township, by then known as New Whatcom, consolidated with the neighboring town of Fairhaven to become the city of Bellingham.

Following Byron's death in 1908, the hotel was sold to Leopold Schmidt, owner of the Schmidt Brewery in Tumwater (which he later renamed the Olympia Brewery). In 1910 Schmidt, who was setting up the Bellingham Bay Brewery at the time, bought the Byron House, which became his home until his death in 1914.

According to the National Register nomination form, during the time of Schmidt's ownership, the Byron House was managed by Henry Schupp, who, after Schmidt's death, renamed the property the Leopold Hotel to honor the man who was his longtime associate, good friend, and employer.

In 1913 the hotel was expanded to 200 rooms (100 with private baths) and a dining room that seated 150 people. Additionally, the rooms now had electrical lights and hot-and-cold running water. In the early 1920s, the hotel expanded again, adding a ballroom (originally called the Tulip Room) that could accommodate as many as 250 guests and, in the fall of 1929, an additional hotel tower that more than doubled the number of rooms.

It is the latter construction that constitutes what remains of the original Leopold Hotel complex (the original section was demolished in 1967 in order to build a motor lodge) and it is this structure that was added to the National Register of Historic Places in 1982.

The nine-story, light brown brick addition, designed by the San Francisco architectural firm H.L. Stevens Company, was constructed in the Mission architectural style with elements of other mid-twenties commercial architectural styles. These touches included round arches over the lower floor windows and a belt course above the top floor and above the third-floor windows.

Throughout the first part of the 20th century, the Leopold was considered one of the most elegant hotels in Bellingham, particularly popular with visiting travelers, according to historical accounts. In the early 1930s, the Leopold was sold to John C. Pierce, who would continue to own it for the next two decades. Since then, ownership of the property has changed hands several times. In 1979 it was acquired by R. Wayne Benson, who, using photographs and the original blueprints, restored it to its original appearance.

During the 1980s, the hotel was converted into a retirement home. However, in 2018, it was sold again and underwent another renovation to convert it back into a hotel with apartments. Reopened in November 2019, it now offers thirty-one hotel rooms along with nine residential apartment suites, a gym, a recreational room, and a library.

The historic "Hotel Leo" in Bellingham once hosted the likes of President William H. Taft and film star Clark Gable.

6
Whatcom Museum of History and Art

48.4510° N, 122.2848° W

On Prospect Street in downtown Bellingham

Looking at the magnificent Whatcom Museum of History and Art in downtown Bellingham, it's understandable why it was the first building in the state of Washington to be placed on the National Register of Historic Places. With its signature center clock tower flanked by four smaller spires, the red-brick-and-sandstone structure, erected in 1892, is a vision of late Victorian-era splendor.

The structure wasn't initially built to serve as a museum. Rather, its original use was as the new city hall building following the merger of the townships of Whatcom and Sehome in 1891, which formed a new community known as New Whatcom. The Whatcom City Council had originally met in the Whatcom County Courthouse and, after that became too crowded, moved into the Oakland Block building, which also housed a hotel, a clothing store, and a sheet-music shop.

New Whatcom civic leaders soon came to believe that, as the then-fourth-largest city in the state, the community deserved a more prestigious city hall that clearly indicated it was a community of substance. In November 1891, the city council hired local architect Alfred Lee to design and build a new civic center on a bluff overlooking Bellingham Bay.

During construction, however, the nation and the state of Washington experienced an economic downturn that resulted in portions of the building remaining unfinished. Additionally, they lacked the funds to purchase the expensive internal mechanism for the tower clock, so the clock's hands were positioned permanently at seven o'clock. Despite an unfinished interior and non-working clock, the new city hall officially opened on May 9, 1893.

The building was eventually completed (although a working clock was never installed) and served as the seat of city government—even after New Whatcom merged in 1904 with the town of Fairhaven to form Bellingham—until 1939. That year, city officials decided they needed additional space for city staff and services and began the process of relocating city operations to a new, more modernist building designed by Bellingham architect Leonard W. Bindon. The new Art Deco-style city hall was built using federal funds from the Public Works Administration and Federal Works Agency programs that were part of the New Deal.

As for Old City Hall, as it became known, the grand Victorian structure became a county museum in 1941. This followed an extensive campaign by local resident John M. Edson to establish a public museum there. Along with leading that effort, Edson, a journalist as well as an amateur scientist and collector, donated his large ornithology collection, which included some 600 mounted birds, to the museum to be displayed. In 1944 the previously independent museum successfully petitioned to become an official city-owned and operated agency, which provided it with long-term financial stability.

The building was severely damaged in 1962, when an electrical fire nearly destroyed the roof and the center clock tower and cupola. The museum remained closed for nearly a decade while funds were raised to renovate and rebuild the damaged parts of the building. In 1974 the museum, which had been placed on the National Register four years earlier, was formally reopened to the public.

In more recent years, the museum, which counts more than 30,000 items in its collections, has expanded to include the Lightcatcher building (opened in 2009) at 205 Flora Street, and the Syre Education Center. The latter is adjacent to the museum in what was formerly a fire station built in 1926. It houses the museum's extensive photo archive (more than 200,000 photographs).

Formerly the Bellingham City Hall, the Whatcom Museum, built in 1892, is one of the finest examples of the late Victorian architctural style that was prevalent in civic buildings in the late 19th century.

7
Peace Arch

49.0021° N, 122.7565° W

On the United States-Canada Border, between Blaine, WA, and Surrey, BC

In 1814 the United States and Great Britain signed the Treaty of Ghent, which ended the War of 1812 and established the formal boundary between America and Canada, which was then part of the British Empire. The treaty marked the end of hostilities between the U.S. and its northern neighbor and the beginning of more than two centuries of peaceful coexistence. Perhaps the most significant proof of that friendship is the fact that the 3,000-mile boundary between the countries has remained the longest undefended border in the world.

In advance of the centennial of the treaty, talks began to establish some type of symbol to commemorate a century of peaceful relations between the U.S. and Canada. Unfortunately, the first World War was raging in Europe at the time, so then-President Woodrow Wilson requested that any commemorative activities be postponed until hostilities concluded.

Following the conclusion of the war, the idea for a treaty centennial celebration again began to gain momentum. Among those supportive of such an effort was Washington businessman Sam Hill, president of the Pacific Highway Association and active with the national Good Roads Association. Hill became so committed to the project that he purchased property in Washington and Canada for the project and would eventually pay for much of the construction.

Once the idea of a commemorative structure was accepted, Hill turned to noted famed American architect Harvey Wiley Corbett, who had designed Bush Tower in New York as well as portions of Rockefeller Center, to design it. Corbett, who declined any payment for his work, developed the blueprints for the Peace Arch, a flat-topped, bipedal structure that was 67 feet tall with a base that was 56-by-29 feet. The arch would be built of concrete (800 yards) and steel (50 tons), with 76 14-inch pilings driven 25 feet deep into the ground.

It would be positioned diagonally, with half of the Peace Arch located on the American side of the border and half on the Canadian side. Construction began in 1920 and the massive white arch was completed less than a year later. To further signify the close relationship between the two countries, a bronze tablet with the image of the *Mayflower* was placed on the outer wall of the American leg of the arch, while a similar tablet with the image of the *Beaver*, the first steam-powered vessel to navigate the Pacific Ocean, was attached to the outer wall of the Canadian leg.

Initially, a piece of the *Mayflower* was placed inside a small container beneath the American plaque and a piece of the *Beaver* was placed in a matching container underneath the Canadian plaque. The historic ship pieces, however, began to decay, and in 1985 they were removed so they could be better preserved in a more suitable location.

Inscribed on the top cross-piece on the Canadian side of the arch are the words, "Brethren Dwelling Together in Unity," while on the American side are the words, "Children of a Common Mother." Inside the 19-foot passage through the arch's center are two iron gates that are open and permanently fastened to the walls. Atop one of the gates are the words, "1814 – Open One Hundred Years – 1914" and over the other are the words, "May These Gates Never Be Closed."

The Peace Arch, which was listed on the National Register in 1996, was formally dedicated on September 6, 1921.

News accounts said that more than 10,000 people attended the event, including government officials from the U.S and Canada, as well as British royalty.

Surrounding the giant arch are matching international parks, several acres in size, that are maintained by the respective governments. The gardens feature large lawns, cedar and alder trees, assorted bushes, and a total of 27 flower beds containing 25,000 flowers, predominately roses, tulips, and dahlias. Lanes of busy Interstate 5 pass incongruously on either side of the arch.

The grand Peace Arch has, since it was completed in 1921, celebrated the special bond between the United States and Canada.

The Seattle skyline viewed from Kerry Park

WEST

The part of Washington surrounded by Puget Sound is often referred to by those living on the east side of the Cascades as the "West Side." It encompasses King, Pierce, and Thurston Counties and includes the cities of Seattle, Tacoma, and Olympia. Commonly known as the Seattle metropolitan area, it is ranked the 15th largest metro area in the U.S., with more than 4 million people. In addition to its myriad cultural happenings and historical sites, Seattle is home to a number of major professional sports teams, including the Seahawks in football, the Mariners in baseball, the Kraken in hockey, the Sounders and Reign FC in men's and women's soccer, the Storm in women's basketball, and the Seawolves in rugby.

The city can trace its roots to September 1851, when three men, David Denny, John Low, and Lee Terry, arrived in a ship commanded by Captain Robert C. Fay at the mouth of the Duwamish River (which flows into Puget Sound). The trio had come to the region to scout locations for a future settlement. They were welcomed by Chief Sealth (later anglicized to "Chief Seattle"), leader of the Duwamish and Suquamish people.

Denny was impressed with the area and wrote a brief letter to his older brother, Arthur, who was recovering from an illness in Portland. It said, "We have examined the valley of the Duwamish river and find it a fine country. There is plenty of room for one thousand settlers. Come at once."

In November 1851, the schooner *Exact* anchored near Alki Beach (now West Seattle) and members of what became known as the Denny party disembarked. In addition to Arthur Denny, the group included 9 other adults and 12 children. The settlers, with the help of Chief Sealth, who had come to believe that cooperation with the whites would lead to peaceful co-existence with them, built a cabin for shelter during the winter.

In the spring, most of the Denny party relocated near the shore of Elliot Bay, at what is now Pioneer Square in downtown Seattle. These pioneers are credited with being among the founders of the city of Seattle. Interestingly, the site was originally known as Dewamps, from a native word for the area. However, in May 1853, when Arthur Denny, another member of his party, Carson Boren, and David "Doc" Maynard, who had come later, filed a townsite plan, they decided to call their new settlement Seattle, in honor of their benefactor Chief Sealth.

Tacoma, located about 34 miles south of Seattle, was established in 1872 and soon became the western terminus of the Northern Pacific Railway, which ran from Minnesota to Puget Sound. Within a short time, it became in important shipping center for Washington's lumber, coal, and wheat industries.

Olympia, about 30 miles south of Tacoma, was founded in the 1850s as a port city and in 1853 was designated as the capital of the newly created Washington Territory. In 1889, when the state of Washington was admitted into the union, Olympia was named its new state capital.

8
Fort Nisqually

47.3034° N, 122.5323° W

On Five Mile Drive in Tacoma's Port Defiance Park

Fort Nisqually has the distinction of being the first European settlement on Puget Sound. In 1832 Archibald McDonald, chief trader for the Hudson's Bay Company (HBC), the most important fur-trading enterprise in the Pacific Northwest, built a crude log cabin warehouse and trading post on the site. Erected on a beach and plain above the Nisqually River Delta, it was known as Nisqually House.

About a year later, HBC had McDonald and a crew of eight men expand the facility by building a fort around the outpost. The location was selected because not only was the Nisqually House already there, but it was halfway between two existing major outposts: Fort Vancouver on the Columbia River and Fort Langley on the Fraser River in British Columbia, Canada.

The site also was near the mouth of Sequalitchew Creek, overlooking the Nisqually River Valley (in the present-day town of DuPont); the creek flowed into Puget Sound and provided ready access to the sea. The site also offered plenty of grassland for grazing cattle and good soil for growing crops, and the HBC was on friendly terms with the local native tribes.

Within a few years, Fort Nisqually grew into an important regional trading post with a decidedly international flavor. Operated by Scotsmen, it was served by workers from Hawaii, the West Indies, Canada, England, America, and other parts of the world.

In 1843 the original fort was replaced by a newer fort, located about a mile away. This new encampment, which was completed that year, included a granary, a blacksmith's shop, a cabin, a saw pit, and the Chief Factor's House (for the manager of the fort's operations), which was built in 1855. On the fertile lands outside the fort, the company developed the first large-scale farm in the Pacific Northwest (more than 160,000 acres). Within a few years, the fort's trade in farm products, including cured meats, surpassed its fur business.

In 1846 the English government relinquished to the United States government its claims to all territory below the 49th parallel. The Fort Nisqually compound, however, remained under the control of the Hudson's Bay Company and its subsidiary, the Puget Sound Agricultural Company. British ownership of such a large swath of land, however, remained a contentious issue between Britain and the U.S. for the next several decades. Then in 1869 the U.S. government purchased the holdings of both the Hudson's Bay Company and the Puget Sound Agricultural Company.

Edward Huggins, the last Chief Factor of Fort Nisqually, became an American citizen and homesteaded the land where the fort stood. He sold the land in 1906 to the DuPont Powder Company, which constructed a black-powder manufacturing facility on the site. By the early 1930s, nearly all of Fort Nisqually's original structures had disappeared due to neglect.

To preserve the two remaining structures, the Chief Factor's House (the oldest extent frame house in Washington) and the granary (the oldest extent building in Washington), the Young Men's Business Club of Tacoma, a civic group, relocated the structures to Tacoma's Point Defiance Park in 1934. The buildings were restored and housed within a reconstruction of the original fort.

Today, the complex, known as the Fort Nisqually Living History Museum, provides a look at one of Washington's earliest

The restored Chief Factor's House at Fort Nisqually in Tacoma's Point Defiance Park, built in 1855, is the oldest frame house in the state.

The preserved granary building at Fort Nisqually in Tacoma's Point Defiance Park, constructed in 1843, is the oldest structure in the state.

communities. In addition to informative exhibits, the museum offers self-guided and group tours, immersive weekends, blacksmith demonstrations, workshops, and other programs.

The Chief Factor's house, along with the granary building (which is considered the only surviving example in the U.S. of the HBC's unique Canadian method of log cabin construction), were declared National Historic Landmarks and listed on the National Register of Historic Places in 1970. In 1974 the original site of Fort Nisqually in DuPont was also added to the National Register.

9
Stadium High School
(STADIUM-SEMINARY HISTORIC DISTRICT)

47.2660° N, 122.4485° W

On North E Street in Tacoma

There is definitely something awesome about a high school that looks like a giant French chateau and served as the setting for a hugely successful late-1990s movie. The place in question is Tacoma's iconic Stadium High School, which was featured prominently in the 1999 film *10 Things I Hate About You*, starring Heath Ledger and Julia Stiles.

Perhaps not surprising given it looks more like a fancy resort than a typical high school, the building was originally intended to be a luxury resort called the Olympic (or Tourist) Hotel. In 1891 the Tacoma Land Company hired famed Philadelphia architects George Wattson Hewitt and William Dempster Hewitt, who were brothers, to design a luxury hotel that would cater to passengers traveling on the transcontinental Northern Pacific Railway (NPR), for which Tacoma was the western terminus.

Unfortunately, just as the hotel was being built, the nation suffered a national economic downturn, which became known as the Panic of 1893. This national depression, which lasted until about 1897, resulted in the railroad being taken over by new owners, who decided to abandon the hotel project.

For the next few years, the structure, which would later become known as the "Brown Castle," was used as a lumber and shingle warehouse by the railroad. In 1898 a fire severely damaged the building. After the railroad announced plans to demolish the structure and salvage the bricks, the Tacoma School Board stepped forward to purchase it in 1903 for a new high school.

The school district hired Tacoma architect Frederick Henry Heath to rebuild the structure and add a large bowl-shaped stadium in a place known as "Old Woman's Gulch," directly north and east of the building. According to historical records, the gulch derived its name from the widows who lived in shacks along the bottom of the gully there.

His design incorporated the French Chateauesque and Romanesque Revival styles of the original structure, which can be seen in the use of turrets, parapets, dormer windows, arched doorways and windows, and decorative brickwork.

The construction, which cost $500,000 (or about $17.6 million in today's dollars), began in 1904 and was completed in 1906, while the adjacent Stadium Bowl, with a seating capacity of 32,000, was finished three years later. The stadium was used for football games and track events, hosted sports celebrities like Babe Ruth, who put on a batting exhibition and Jack Dempsey, who sparred for a charity event, and was the site where speeches were given by three US presidents, Theodore Roosevelt, Warren G. Harding, and Franklin D. Roosevelt.

Originally called Tacoma High School, the school's name was changed to Stadium High School in 1913 (in fact, the surrounding neighborhood is known as the Stadium-Seminary Historic District). In 1977 it was added to the National Register of Historic Places as part of the historic district. Over the years, the school and stadium have been renovated and expanded. In the 1970s and 1980s, the stadium was reduced in size due to structural concerns and flood damage. In 2006 the school was given a seismic upgrade and underwent significant historical renovation.

With its stately French chateau appearance, Tacoma's Stadium High School is among the most beautiful education facilities in Washington state.

10
Washington State Capitol Complex

47.3034° N, 122.5323° W

On Sid Snyder Avenue SW on a bluff overlooking downtown Olympia

It took several tries to build Washington's current capitol building. After Washington Territory was created in 1853, the territorial government held it first meetings in a room above the Gold Bar Restaurant in downtown Olympia. The second and third gatherings of that group took place in Olympia's Masonic Hall (neither the Gold Bar nor the Masonic Hall remain standing).

In 1855 Edmund Sylvester, Olympia's founder, donated to the state 12 acres on a bluff overlooking the town for a more permanent home. Territorial officials accepted the gift and approved funding for a two-story, 40-by-80-foot wooden structure that resembled a New England church (sans steeple), which was completed in 1856.

That first capitol, however, was too small to house all of the agencies when the state of Washington was established in 1889, and lawmakers began planning a new capitol building. In 1893 the foundations for a new capitol were laid near the site of the first one. The rest of the work wasn't completed, however, because the allocated funds ran out. In 1902 state officials changed course and decided to abandon the unfinished project and purchase the recently completed Thurston County Courthouse in downtown Olympia for $350,000 and add a $500,000 annex.

Now known as the Old State Capitol Building, the renovated and expanded structure was completed in 1905 and served as the home of Washington's state government operations for the next two decades. But by 1911, it had become apparent that the former courthouse was also too small for the needs of the growing state, so the legislature approved a plan to build a new capitol on the site of the original capitol building, incorporating the completed foundation.

Funding for this third capitol complex was approved in 1919 and work began on the project in 1922. The completed foundation wasn't large enough to provide enough space to accommodate all state agencies, so the plans for the new capitol, designed by architects Walter R. Wilder and Harry K. White of New York, called for building a complex with several buildings. The structure built on the completed foundation became the Legislative Building, which was finished in 1928. This massive, domed building was and is the centerpiece of the Capitol Campus. It houses not only the legislative branches of government but executive offices, including that of the Governor.

Erected adjacent to the Legislative Building were the Temple of Justice, completed in 1920, to house the Washington Supreme Court, and the Insurance Building, completed in 1921 to house the state Insurance Commissioner and State Auditor operations. The Capitol Campus plans included additional structures, which were completed later, including the Transportation Building (1937), the Public Health Building (1940), the Pritchard Building (1958), and a handful of others in more recent years. A key element in Wilder and White's capitol campus plan was the landscaping. The firm hired noted landscaping architects, the Massachusetts-based Olmstead Brothers, to design expansive green spaces, circular pathways, and lush vegetation to create a true park-like setting.

Over the years, several noteworthy monuments and sculptures have been added to the campus, including the bronze War Memorial Sculpture, erected in 1938, memorializing those who fought in World War I, and a 71-foot totem pole celebrating Washington's native people, carved by Chief William Shelton of the Snohomish Tribe, which was installed in 1940.

The Washington State Capitol Historic District, which encompasses about 29 acres, was listed on the National Register of Historic Places in 1979.

The Washington State Legislative Building was completed in 1928 and serves as the center of the historic State Capitol Complex in Olympia.

11
Old State Capitol Building

47.0429° N, 122.8995° W

On Washington Street SE in downtown Olympia

It could easily be argued that the Old State Capitol Building in Olympia is a survivor. The two-and-a-half-story, rock-faced, sandstone structure was built in 1891 to serve as the Thurston County Courthouse. Originally an octagonal, 150-foot stone clocktower, with a clock face for each of the eight facets, rose from behind the courthouse, and a dozen smaller conical towers, or turrets, were constructed around all sides of the building. Designed by Washington architect Willis Ritchie, who was also responsible for the Spokane County Courthouse in Spokane and the Jefferson County Courthouse in Port Townsend, the structure incorporated the 19th-century American Romanesque Revival style that was popular at the time.

In 1901 the state of Washington purchased the courthouse from Thurston County to serve as the new state capitol. State offices had outgrown Washington's original capitol, a two-story wood-frame building that had been erected in 1856 as the territorial capitol. Lawmakers also felt the territorial capitol building was too far from downtown Olympia's lodging houses and restaurants.

Renovation of the courthouse, which included adding a rotunda and an annex, wasn't completed until the beginning of the 1905 legislative session. While a vast improvement over the original capitol, which was demolished in 1911, the former courthouse soon proved that it, too, was insufficient for the rapidly growing state. That year, the legislature authorized plans to build a new capitol on the12-acre site of the original territorial capitol. Funds to begin the project weren't approved until 1919 and, following a design competition, work began on the new capitol in 1923. It would be completed five years later.

As for the old structure, now known as the Old Capitol Building, it continued to be used by a number of state offices and has been modified several times over the years. In 1928 a fire broke out that gutted the clock tower, which had to be removed, and damaged the upper floors of the structure. During reconstruction of the building, which took nearly a decade, the height of the second-floor chamber, which had once served as the home of the state legislature, was reduced, and the building was equipped with new boilers and a steam-pipe heating system.

In 1949 an earthquake severely damaged the structure, including the loss of 10 of the 12 exterior turrets and the rotunda. It was repaired, including the turrets, and retrofitted with internal steel reinforcements and additional bracing. The most recent renovation of the structure occurred in 1982, when new plaster was applied to the interior walls, new ceilings were put in, a skylight and copper roof were added, and two modern elevators were installed in the building.

The Old Capitol Building, which has been the home of the Office of the Superintendent of Public Instruction since 1905 (one of several state agencies housed in the building during its time as a state capital), was added to the National Register of Historic Places in 1975.

Originally built to serve as the Thurston County Courthouse, this castle-like structure in downtown Olympia served as the Washington State Capitol from 1905 to 1928.

12
Nihon Go Gakko
(JAPANESE LANGUAGE SCHOOL)

47.5977° N, 122.3120° W

On South Weller Street in downtown Seattle

The Nihon Go Gakko (or Kokugo Gakko), also known as the Japanese Language School, was established in the early 20th century to ensure that Japanese history, culture, and language would be passed on to future generations of Japanese Americans. It is the oldest Japanese language school in the continental U.S. and was one of about two dozen such schools operating in the state of Washington in the 1930s.

Immigrants from Japan, many of whom originally settled in Oregon, began migrating to Seattle in the late 19th century. Most were hired to work in the city's fisheries, in sawmills, and on its railroads, but their number also included students, merchants, and farmers. While only about 125 Japanese citizens lived in Seattle in 1890, by 1900 there were 3,900 residing in the city.

Many of these new arrivals brought with them their home country's traditions and way of life, and believed it important to educate their American-born children and grandchildren in the customs and values of Japan. To meet this need, a series of Japanese language schools began to appear in the western U.S. communities that had significant Japanese populations, including Seattle and San Francisco.

In Seattle, the first school opened its doors in 1902 on the second floor of a Japanese-owned business, the Furuya Company. Eight years later, it relocated to the basement of a Buddhist church. Finally, in 1913, the school moved into what would become its permanent home, a simple two-story wooden building with a pedimented entry on South Weller Street. A second, nearly identical structure, adjacent to the first, was added in 1917, and a third, smaller building was completed in 1920. This final addition was set behind the other two and is separated from them by an alley. Unlike the others, its entrance is on King Street. All were funded by the local Japanese community.

During its first year on South Weller Street, the school had 98 students in its eight primary grades, with additional students taking first- and second-year refresher courses. By the 1920s, following the two expansions, the school had an enrollment of 1,800 in daytime classes. According to records, weekday classes began at 3 p.m., immediately after the end of the public-school day, and continued until 5 p.m., except during the winter, when instructional time was reduced to one hour.

During World War II, the school's buildings were occupied by the U.S. Air Force, which used them as a training facility, Following the conclusion of the war, the school served as a temporary home for Japanese Americans from the Seattle area who had been placed in internment camps during the war.

Today, the Nihon Go Gakko is home of the Japanese Cultural and Community Center, which promotes Japanese culture, including through language classes. In 1982, the school buildings were added to the National Register of Historic Places.

Established in 1902, Nihon Go Gakko in Seattle is the oldest still-functioning Japanese language school in the continental U.S. Its three buildings were constructed between 1913 and 1920.

13
Chinatown-International District

47.5987° N, 122.3240° W

Roughly bounded by Yesler, Rainier, Dearborn, and Fourth Streets in downtown Seattle

Seattle's 23-acre International District, also known as the Chinatown Historic District, has long been a magnet for the city's Asian immigrants. Established in the late 19th century, the 16-block area is a neighborhood consisting of a variety of ethnic groups, including Chinese, Japanese, Filipino, Italian, Native American, and African American residents.

The first Chinese immigrants to settle in Seattle arrived in the 1860s and 1870s, when Chinese laborers were contracted to work in the region's lumber mills and fishing operations as well as to build its railroads. To house these workers, who were mostly single men, Chinese businessmen, who often served as middlemen to bring the workers into the country, constructed boardinghouses in the tidal flats south of Pioneer Square and the docks, adjacent to a steam sawmill owned by future Seattle mayor Henry Yesler. These were built on stilts over the flats.

By the 1870s, an estimated 550 people lived in the neighborhood. The Great Seattle Fire of 1889, however, destroyed nearly all the buildings. Following the disaster, wealthy Chinese businessman Chin Gee Hee constructed a solid brick structure, known as the Canton Building, at 208 South Washington Street (east of the current International District). The building served as the catalyst for the development of a new Chinatown area.

In 1907 the city of Seattle began what has become known as the Jackson Street Regrade, essentially the removal of some 85 feet of soil from a hill at the top of Jackson Street, then using the dirt for fill in the tidal flats. The earth-moving was part of a massive project to make Seattle more level and accessible, and thus easier to develop. The Jackson Street Regrade, which took about three years, reshaped more than 100 blocks in downtown Seattle, including the uprooting of the new Chinatown. Residents and businesses relocated to nearby King Street on land reclaimed by the fill from the regrade. The result was the development of Seattle's third Chinatown district.

The national Chinese Exclusion Act of 1882 effectively slowed the growth of Washington's Chinese population. Since American businesses, especially in the agricultural field, continued to need immigrant workers, the result was a rapid increase in Japanese immigrants, who were not affected by the national immigration restrictions placed on the Chinese.

By the early 1900s, the Japanese had become Seattle's largest minority population, with many residing in the neighborhood to the north and east of Chinatown, in what came to be called "Japantown." Other ethnic groups also began to arrive, including substantial numbers of Filipinos, who established businesses and built homes south of Chinatown in an area that became known as "Manilatown."

During World War II, residents of Japantown were forced by the American government to abandon their homes and businesses and sent to live in the Minidoka Relocation Center in Idaho. When large numbers of African American workers came to Seattle for military duty or to fill wartime jobs, many moved into the abandoned buildings and homes in Japantown. One result was the development of several clubs and dancehalls along South Jackson Street, which soon became known for blues, jazz, and swing music. Following the war, many of the previous Japanese residents of Japantown chose not to return to Seattle or settled in other parts of the city.

In the mid-20th century, the building of Interstate 5 created a physical division between the different Asian neighborhoods

The entrance to Seattle's 23-acre International District, also known as the Chinatown Historic District, is marked by a 45-foot-tall Paifang-style entry gate, built in 2007, at 5th Avenue and King Street.

in the district and resulted in the destruction of a large number of Asian-owned businesses, churches, and housing units. Additionally, in the 1970s, the construction of the Kingdome Stadium, on the southwestern edge of the Chinatown district, created increased traffic and parking issues for the area, which negatively impacted local businesses and residents. Additionally, the approval of stricter Seattle building and safety codes at that time meant demolishing some of the district's older structures, many of which provided affordable housing.

The adoption of Seattle's International Special Review District in 1973, which recognized the importance of preserving the neighborhood's Asian culture and history, began to slow the destruction of the city's Asian district. Since then, the city and neighborhood have protected the area from unwanted development and sought to preserve the neighborhood's character. The city also completed several redevelopment projects, including the creation of Hing Hay Park, which boasts a large Chinese pavilion—a gift of the people of Taipei, Taiwan—as well as the construction of a 45-foot-tall entry gate to the district (located at 5th Avenue and King Street). Newer civic projects include Kobe Terrace Park, home of the Danny Woo International District Community Garden, the Wing Luke Museum of the Asian Pacific American Experience, and Uwajimaya Village (pronounced "Oo-Gee-My-Uh"), a mixed-use commercial and residential development that includes the popular Uwajimaya Asian Market.

In 1986 the district, which includes 50 historic buildings ranging from hotels and apartment houses to commercial buildings and automobile garages, was placed on the National Register of Historic Places.

14
Pike Place Public Market Historic District

47.5987° N, 122.3240° W

On Pike Street in downtown Seattle

Seattle's skyline has definitely changed in recent years. New gleaming metal-and-glass towers have cropped up throughout the city core almost overnight and it seems as if construction cranes have become permanent fixtures in the city. Yet in spite of the rapid changes, one of the city's landmarks—the Pike Place Public Market—has somehow managed to survive and thrive for more than a century. With its stalls of vendors selling fresh fish, flowers, produce, herbs, baked goods, crafts, and antiques, the market harkens back to an earlier time.

It is that direct connection with the city's past, in fact, that has made the Pike Place Market the most popular tourism destination in Seattle. It is one of the oldest continuously operated public farmers' markets in the country. The market, which has been modified extensively over the decades, began as a farmers' street market on a portion of land known as Pike Place, above the Elliott Bay tide flats off Pike Street and First Avenue. Primarily a produce market, farmers initially sold their wares from wagons they parked on the street.

In November 1907, however, the first permanent building (a long, narrow shed known as the Main Arcade) was erected on the site to protect vendors and customers from Seattle's typical rainy weather. During the next decade and a half, the market expanded with the construction of more substantial, interconnected buildings, including the Corner Market, the Economy Market, the Sanitary Market, and the lower levels of the Main Market.

During this time a number of other market buildings, including several small hotels and lodging houses, were built in the district. These included the Outlook Hotel, the Cliff House, and the Leland Hotel. By the late 1920s, some 600 farmers, many of whom were Japanese American, held permits to sell at the market, which attracted about 25,000 shoppers on an average weekday. But during World War II, the forced internment of most Japanese Americans on the West Coast caused the market to lose many of its suppliers, and the market began to decline. After the war, few of the formerly interred Seattleites returned, having lost their property. By the late 1950s, the market's shoppers largely consisted of tourists and elderly and low-income residents living downtown.

In 1963, partly because of the market's deterioration, it became part of the city's urban redevelopment plans. A citizens' group, Friends of the Market, soon formed to fight this effort to close and replace the market. In 1971 the group successfully passed a city ballot initiative that created a special historic district to protect the market and its surrounding buildings.

Also in the early 1970s, the city, which had purchased 14 buildings within the district, established the nonprofit Pike Place Market Preservation and Development Authority to serve as the market's property manager and as steward of the privately owned buildings in the district.

In subsequent years, the city, using local urban renewal or federal Housing and Urban Development funding, embarked on a number of rehabilitation projects to improve and preserve more than two dozen buildings within the district and create public spaces for the market. As part of these efforts, Pike Street was reconstructed using traditional cobblestone paving and granite curbs.

More recently, the nonprofit Pike Place Foundation was formed to raise funds for and administer the market's free health clinic, senior center, low-income housing, food bank, and childcare center and preschool. An estimated 500 residents currently live within the historic district.

The Pike Place Public Market (originally encompassing only one and a half acres) was added to the National Register of Historic Places in 1972. The listing was expanded in 2011 to include additional historic sites, bringing the total size of the historic district to seven acres.

The iconic outdoor sign on Seattle's Pike Place Public Market, which has been an important downtown retail center in the city since 1907.

15
King Street Station

47.5984° N, 122.3299° W

On King Street in downtown Seattle

At the turn of the 20th century, when businessman James J. Hill, who controlled both the Great Northern Railway and the Northern Pacific Railway Company, decided to build a new depot where the two lines met in downtown Seattle, he looked to Italy for inspiration. Hill's companies' previous depot was a modest wooden structure on Railroad Avenue, erected by the Northern Pacific following the Great Seattle fire of 1889. The new station would be grander and more befitting of a rising new city—and a prosperous railroad company.

Hill's plan was to construct this monument to progress on reclaimed tidelands. To bring trains to the station, Hill and city officials devised an ingenious plan to bore a 5,245-foot tunnel underneath downtown Seattle, which eliminated congestion from passenger traffic blocking the adjacent waterfront area. The tunnel, completed in 1904, is still in use.

The new brick station was designed to echo the original campanile in the Piazza de San Marco in Venice, Italy. Built in a style many architects have described as "Railroad Italianate," the depot incorporates a variety of architectural influences including Beaux Arts, Neoclassical, Commercial, and Italian Renaissance. It boasted an elegant clock tower rising from a multistory rectangular structure. The clock in the tower, which is actually a single mechanism with four faces, is the work of Boston's E. Howard & Co., who also created the large clocks for San Francisco's Ferry Building and Chicago's Wrigley Building.

In addition to the 242-foot clock tower, which made the depot Seattle's tallest building at the time, the ground floor boasted high, ornamental plaster ceilings along with plaster walls and fluted Corinthian columns. The lower portion of the walls and the columns had white marble accents with white, green, and gold glass mosaic tiles. In the center of the waiting room was a massive bronze chandelier, while four smaller chandeliers and wall sconces provided additional light. The terrazzo floor featured inlaid square mosaic tiles, which formed a compass-shaped pattern near the station entrance and other patterns throughout the rest of the floor.

When it opened in May 1906, the station, with its 14-foot-wide clock faces on four sides, immediately boosted Seattle's image by showing that the city's transportation facilities were equal to any in the nation. Unfortunately, later renovations in the 1940s, '50s, and '60s resulted in the removal of many of the station's original interior design elements, such as the plaster walls, mosaic tiles, and marble accents. The beautiful chandeliers were replaced with industrial fluorescent lights.

By the early 1990s, the station was in sad shape, with the once-fabulous terrazzo floor cracked and in disrepair. The building was also in need of expensive seismic retrofitting. Fortunately, a coalition of local historic preservationists led by the Seattle Historical Society, which had already helped get the station listed on the National Register of Historic Places in 1973, joined with city, state, and federal transportation agencies to renovate the structure.

In 1998 the Washington Department of Transportation, aided by $5 million from Amtrak, began renovations. In 2006

Seattle voters approved Proposition 1, which allocated another $10 million for the station project. Eventually, more than $56 million was raised from a variety of public and private sources to complete the restoration. The newly revamped King Street Station opened in April 2013 before a crowd of more than 500 people, including political dignitaries and a brass band. No doubt James J. Hill would have approved.

With its 242-foot-tall clock tower, Seattle's King Street Station, which opened in 1906, has long been one of the city's most visible landmarks.

16
Washington Hall

47.6028° N, 122.3145° W

On 14th Avenue in downtown Seattle

The Danish Brotherhood in America, Seattle Lodge #29, had no idea that a community hall and boardinghouse they constructed in 1908 for newly arrived Danish immigrants would one day host performances by the likes of singer Billie Holiday, the punk band The Dead Kennedys, and a local high school band with a young guitarist named Jimi Hendrix.

That three-story building, which Lodge #29 named Washington Hall, originally consisted of one-room apartments for new arrivals to Seattle along with meeting space for the brotherhood's members. Designed by noted Seattle architect Victor W. Voorhees, the hall was intended as a multipurpose facility with a large, second-floor dancehall, which could serve as a venue for live performances. This space could be rented and provide additional income for the brotherhood. The apartments were located to the rear of the building. Voorhees' design incorporated Mission Revival and other commercial styles in a wood-frame structure with a brick veneer. Measuring 61-by-128 feet, the rectangular building boasts a distinctive Mission-style parapet painted a bright red on its east side.

From its beginning, Washington Hall opened its doors to not only immigrants from a wide range of ethnic groups, but also to residents of the neighborhood, called Squire Park, which the City of Seattle's Landmarks Preservation Board has described as "constantly fluctuating" over the years. Thus the hall hosted an eclectic variety of events, including the state convention of the Ancient Order of Hibernians (an Irish social group) in 1912, a Purim celebration benefitting the Seattle Talmud Torah and the Bikur Cholim Sunday School in 1921, and a reading by poet Capt. Peter Perunovich, who performed in Serbian. Additionally, in the 1930s the hall hosted twice-monthly meetings of an African American Masonic Lodge, regular meetings and dances of the Seattle Filipino Youth Club, and a banquet and ball honoring the 52nd anniversary of Italian King Victor Emmanuel II's triumphant entry into Rome in 1870, which marked the unification of that country. It later also welcomed a wide variety of political organization meetings and labor union gatherings.

The hall also played an important role as an entertainment venue, hosting what is believed to be the first documented jazz performance by a local ensemble in 1918 (Lillian Smith's Jazz Band played a benefit for the NAACP). By the mid-20th century, the hall had hosted Oscar Holden, Billie Holiday, Duke Ellington and his Orchestra, Mahalia Jackson, Marian Anderson, Count Basie, and, on the evening of February 20, 1960, 17-year-old Jimi Hendrix and his band, The Rockin' Kings.

Over the decades, the hall has been modified several times. The first changes came in the 1920s, when two entryways were altered. Earthquake damage in 1949 required the removal of the south parapet. A fire in 1970 resulted in the destruction of the back apartments. From 1973 to 2007, the building was owned by the Sons of Haiti, an African American Masonic Lodge, who remodeled it several times.

In 2010 the hall was acquired by the City of Seattle's Landmark Preservation Board for $1.5 million. The hall was added to the National Register of Historic Places the same year, and the board began phased-in renovations of the building, which are ongoing.

In recent years, Washington Hall has housed several Seattle arts organizations, including 206 Zulu, which engages youth, low-income people, and people of color in social change through innovative programs involving hip-hop music, arts, and culture; Hidmo, a network of artists, educators, and activists that nurtures community and independent arts endeavors; and Voices Rising, an intergenerational showcase for LGBTQ performers of color.

Originally built in 1908 as a boardinghouse for Danish immigrants, Seattle's Washington Hall later served as a music venue, hosting performers ranging from blues singer Billie Holiday to a young high school guitarist named Jimi Hendrix.

17
Samuel Hyde House

47.6318° N, 122.2845° W

On East Madison Street in Seattle's Madison Park neighborhood

When Seattle businessman Samuel Hyde, who made a fortune in coal mining and with his wholesale liquor company, decided to build a home for his family, he did it with flair. After procuring a half-acre parcel in the tony Madison Park neighborhood near Lake Washington, he hired prominent local architects Charles H. Bebb and Louis L. Mendel to design his residence, which also had a carriage house, brick privacy walls, and manicured gardens. The latter were laid out by the famed Olmsted Brothers, who also designed most of Seattle's parks as well as Central Park in New York and San Francisco's Golden Gate Park.

Bebb and Mendell designed a neoclassical, two-story mansion with a wooden frame and pressed-brick exterior veneer. The entrance portico was highlighted by two pairs of large, Corinthian columns. The house also had a side porte-cochere by which Hyde could access his chauffeur-driven limousine. The interior of the residence, which was constructed between 1909 and 1910, had Tiffany light fixtures, a ceiling mural, stained-glass windows, a marble fireplace, and Siberian oak paneling. When completed, the mansion was considered one of the most elegant in Seattle.

Sadly, Hyde and his wife, Rachel, only resided in the home for about six years. In 1914 Washington voters passed an initiative that outlawed the manufacture and sale of alcoholic beverages, which took effect in 1916. The ban effectively forced Hyde to close his liquor company. The loss of the business also meant the Hydes had to sell their grand house. According to accounts, Hyde decided to devote more attention to his coal-mining investments. He and his wife eventually settled into an apartment on 15th Avenue, about two miles east of their previous house, where they lived until he died in May 1944.

As for the Hyde House, it passed through several owners during the next several decades before it was placed on the National Historic Register in 1982. In the early 1990s, it was purchased by the Russian government to use as a consular residence (Russia's only consulate on the West Coast). Under the terms of the sale, the Russian government became owners of the building, while the U.S. government owned the land on which it sat. Over the years, the house hosted trade and business meetings, diplomatic parties, and other consulate events.

However, in 2018, President Donald Trump ordered the expulsion of 60 Russian diplomats in the U.S., all of whom were stationed at the Hyde House. The house was ordered shuttered and placed in the custody of the U.S. State Department. According to the *Capitol Hill Seattle* news site, the closure was the result of an alleged Kremlin-backed nerve-agent attack in England. The site said the diplomats living in Seattle had been identified as intelligence agents who may have been spying on local military contractors such as Boeing and Microsoft, as well as several nearby military bases.

Since then, the stately home has stood vacant. U.S. government officials have changed all the locks and placed it under the supervision of a security staff, and they regularly conduct inspections of the house to make sure it remains in good shape. As for the Russians, they have indicated they would like to move back in whenever relations between their country and the U.S. are normalized again.

The majestic Samuel Hyde House in Seattle's Madison Park neighborhood was constructed in 1910 for liquor entrepreneur Samuel Hyde, then served for many years as Russia's consulate office.

18
Saint Edward State Park

47.7328° N, 122.2572° W

On Juanita Drive NE in Kenmore

When Seattle's Roman Catholic Bishop Edward John O'Dea first visited the Deer Park property on the northeast shore of Lake Washington in 1925, he immediately knew he had found the site for a new seminary. The serene, wooded area on the banks of the lake was a perfect location for building an institution devoted to training future priests.

O'Dea, in fact, was so convinced it was the right spot that he purchased four parcels totaling 366 acres with money he had inherited (at a reported cost of $81,000 or about $1.4 million in today's dollars) and then donated the property to the diocese for the seminary.

During his tenure, which began in 1890, the bishop—who was the first in the Diocese of Seattle—had greatly expanded the number of Catholic churches, orphanages, and schools in Washington. But with all that expansion came a need for additional priests. And almost from the beginning of his appointment to bishop, O'Dea had wanted to build a seminary in the region.

Once the site was acquired, O'Dea began to raise construction funds. By 1930, he had pulled together more than $100,000 in donations, which was matched by a $200,000 loan taken out by the dioceses. With funding in hand, he hired one of Seattle's most prominent architects, John Graham Sr. (whose firm would later design the Space Needle) to design a facility with 130 individual dormitory rooms, a grand dining hall, a large kitchen and butcher shop, a laundry area, a library, classrooms, laboratories, a study hall, a recreation room, and several chapels.

Desiring to build something appropriately stately and grand, Graham incorporated the Late Romanesque Revival style of architecture, which had become popular at the time for religious structures. The resulting rectangular concrete-and-brick building was four stories tall, with a prominent six-story bell tower. Graham situated the building on a 20-acre clearing on the highest part of the property, which provided a marvelous view of the lake through the surrounding trees. His plans also included a football field, horseshoe pits, and tennis, volleyball, and handball courts.

Construction on the main building was completed in 1931, with the first group of seminarians beginning classes in September of that year. By 1935 the seminary had grown from a 6-year "minor" seminary to a 12-year "major" seminary. It became fully accredited in the late 1930s—the first seminary to be so designated in the U.S.

Additional facilities were added over the years, including a stone grotto and concrete walkways in the late 1940s, a full gymnasium in 1951, and a swimming pool in 1968. A second seminary building, Saint Thomas Seminary, was added in 1958. Located about a quarter-mile from Saint Edward, it would later be sold to Bastyr University.

In the 1970s, enrollment in the seminary had declined to the point that the diocese was forced to shut down the school following graduation in May 1976. The diocese decided to sell 316 acres of the site (excluding the Saint Thomas portion) and reached out to the state of Washington to purchase it for a state park.

State officials were immediately interested in acquiring the last major parcel of largely undeveloped land on Lake Washington and, in 1977, agreed to pay $7 million dollars for the

Now a boutique hotel with gourmet dining called the Lodge at Saint Edward Park, the structure was built in 1930 as a seminary for training Catholic priests.

land and seminary. More than $3 million was raised through a recreational bond issue approved by voters, with the rest provided by the Federal Land and Water Conservation Fund.

The dedication of the new Saint Edward State Park took place on April 16, 1978, with the seminary temporarily converted into a work camp for the Young Adult Conservation Corp. After funding for that program dried up in 1980, the seminary building stood vacant for nearly 40 years. As part of the state's efforts to preserve the structure, it was added to the National Register of Historic Places in 2007.

A decade later, the state entered into a unique public-private partnership with Daniels Real Estate to restore the seminary and transform it into an upscale boutique hotel, known as The Lodge at Saint Edward Park. The renovated property, which has 84 guestrooms, meeting spaces, a full ballroom, a gourmet restaurant, and a bar, opened in 2021.

19
Snoqualmie Falls

47.5417° N, 121.8377° W

On Railroad Avenue SE in Snoqualmie

Snoqualmie Falls is far more than just a place to snap pretty photographs. The falls, in fact, play an important role in the creation stories for the native Snoqualmie people, who have lived in the area for thousands of years.

According to the Snoqualmie, many years ago two sisters came to the area to dig for fern roots. When night came, they decided to rest. As they lay looking at the stars, one of the sisters made a wish that a shining white star would become her husband while a shining red star would become her sister's spouse.

When the two awoke the next day, they found themselves lying next to the men of their dreams. For a time, the sisters lived in the sky with their husbands, with the older one giving birth to a demigod son, whom they named Moon (later known as Moon the Transformer). But one day while digging for roots, the sisters saw that if they dug straight down they could see their home below. Feeling homesick, they crafted a ladder, carefully closed the hole in the sky, and, with Moon in tow, climbed down to earth, where they were warmly greeted by their people, who did not know where they had disappeared.

During the celebrations, however, a creature called Dog Salmon stole Moon. The sisters called upon several of the birds, including Raven and Osprey, to find the child. Finally, Bluejay spotted Moon, now a grown man with children of his own, living with Dog Salmon's people. After learning his history from Bluejay, Moon decided to leave. As he started up the river, he drove Dog Salmon and his people ahead of him, saying they shall become food for his own people.

When Moon reached the place where Snoqualmie Falls are today, he recognized it as the place where he had been stolen. At that time, the river ended at a fish weir of wood, which prevented the salmon from moving upstream. Moon transformed the fish weir into a waterfall and declared the place would henceforth be where birds, deer, and other game would be abundant enough to feed his people.

He also began creating the various tribes of the region as well as the rivers, including the Puyallup and the Nisqually, in which he placed fish and which he surrounded with plentiful game. Thus, according to the Snoqualmie, Moon was responsible for the creation of the native people and for providing their means of sustenance.

In 2015, in testimony to the U.S. House Appropriations Subcommittee on Interior and Related Agencies, Carolyn Lubenau, former chair of the Snoqualmie Indian Tribe, testified that the falls are sacred to her people.

"It was Moon the Transformer who created our Sacred Snoqualmie Falls," she said. "The mists rising from the powerful cascading waters were created so our prayers could be carried by the mists up to the Creator. The Falls and the area around the Falls have always been used as ceremonial grounds and the surrounding areas are our burial sites, where souls are returned to the Creator and reside forever in our memories. The spirit of the Snoqualmie Falls is there to strengthen, heal and renew us. The Falls is the center of who we are as a people."

It is because of the essential role the falls have played in the lives and culture of the Snoqualmie that it was designated a Traditional Cultural Property and placed on the National Historic Register in 2009.

Beautiful Snoqualmie Falls has long been an important rendezvous spot for local and regional indigenous tribes.

While the falls are sacred, they are open to the public. From a parking lot adjacent to the Salish Lodge & Spa (a luxury hotel and restaurant built above the falls and now owned by the Snoqualmie Tribe), visitors can head to several spots that offer magnificent views of the 268-foot-tall falls. The easiest is an overlook observation area near the parking lot. Perhaps the best views, however, can be found at the end of a short (1.4-mile) but steep trail that leads to a second observation area at the base of the falls.

While not readily apparent, the falls are also home to an innovative underground hydroelectric power generator facility developed at the turn of the 20th century. The first plant, constructed in 1898 (and expanded in 1905), is located in an underground chamber immediately upstream of the falls. A second plant, located about a quarter-mile downstream of the falls, was constructed in 1910 and expanded in the late 1950s.

According to the Snoqualmie Falls' National Register of Historic Places nomination, despite the construction of the generators, "the view is largely unchanged from a century before, and the majesty of the Falls, the roar of its current, the mist rising from the pool, and the mossy cliffs which rise on three sides still convey the traditional setting of a site which has played a continuous role in the culture of the Snoqualmie people."

A view of the garden at Fort Vancouver

SOUTHWEST

The part of Washington that borders Oregon and the Pacific Ocean includes some of the most historic sites in the state. For example, Fort Vancouver, established in 1825 by the Hudson's Bay Company on the north bank of the Columbia River (across from modern-day Portland, Oregon), has the distinction of being the oldest non-indigenous settlement in the state.

In addition, explorers Meriwether Lewis and William Clark and their Corps of Discovery traveled through this area during their expedition to reach the Pacific Ocean in November 1805 (they did reach it at the mouth of the Columbia River, near what today is known as Cape Disappointment in Washington).

The first non-natives to visit the site of the present-day city of Vancouver, Washington are believed to have been members of an American ship, the *Columbia Rediviva*, captained by Robert Gray, in 1792. Gray is credited with naming the Columbia River (after his ship). In November of that year, a second boat, a British longboat commanded by Capt. William Broughton under the direction of Capt. George Vancouver (namesake for the city), traveled up the Columbia River into the Columbia Gorge as part of a mapping expedition on behalf of England.

In March 1825, Fort Vancouver was completed by members of the Hudson's Bay Company, a London-based fur-trading enterprise. The fort was situated on grasslands that traditionally had been inhabited by the Klickitat people. It served as the Hudson's Bay Company's main trading post with local native people, as well as the regional administrative headquarters and a main supply post for its fur-trading business.

The Oregon Treaty in 1846 established the 49th parallel as the boundary between the U.S. and Canada. This placed Fort Vancouver on the American side of the boundary. The Hudson's Bay Company relocated its headquarters to Vancouver Island in British Columbia and transferred the fort property to the U.S. Army. By 1849 the Army had built the Vancouver Barracks at Fort Vancouver, setting up the site as the first U.S. Army base in the Pacific Northwest.

In 1860 the Hudson's Bay Company, which had continued to maintain that it had a legal claim to the land around the fort, lost that fight when a U.S. surveyor formally declared it was under the control of the United States and approved subdividing the land. It was from this survey that the city of Vancouver (originally called Columbia City) came into being.

20
Fort Vancouver National Historic Site

45.6258° N, 122.6585° W

On East 5th Street in Vancouver

Laid out on a plain above the Columbia River, with unobstructed views of the river in both directions, Fort Vancouver was an ideal place on which to place a secure military compound and trading post. It also had been occupied for thousands of years by the indigenous Klickitat people.

In 1824 Sir George Simpson, the highest-ranking administrator in North America for the Hudson's Bay Company from 1820 to 1860, selected the site for the company's headquarters for the Pacific Northwest, Idaho, and British Columbia. Soon a stockade was constructed, which is now known as the first Fort Vancouver (named to honor explorer Capt. George Vancouver). In 1825, after a visit to the fort, Simpson predicted that "it will in two years hence be the finest place in North America."

Five years after it was built, the company relocated the fort to a nearby flatter area called Jolie Prairie. The new site, commonly called the second Fort Vancouver, had better pastureland as well as rich soil for planting crops. It also was closer to the river so it provided better access to fresh water and transportation (but was above the flood zone). Dense forests to the west and north offered ready access to timber.

This second fort comprised a tall wooden palisade surrounding more than a dozen wooden buildings. It catered not only to farmers and herders (many of whom lived in a village outside the fort walls) but to the native people, who would trade furs and fish for goods. By the 1840s, the fort had become a hodgepodge of ethnic and cultural groups, including Scots, Englishmen, French Canadians, Irishmen, Hawaiians, and Iroquois, Cree, and Metis people. Accounts at the time note that fort residents and visitors could hear a constant "Babel of languages."

Following the signing of the Oregon Treaty in 1846, Fort Vancouver became part of the United States. The Hudson's Bay Company maintained a small presence at the fort until 1860. Then, after losing a dispute with the U.S. Army, the company agreed to turn over all of the property to the U.S. government and departed. The Army, which had maintained a post near the fort since 1849, took control of the entire facility.

In 1866 the second Fort Vancouver caught fire and was destroyed. A century later, in the mid-1960s, the fort was reconstructed to its original appearance with reproductions of its original buildings. It remains a popular historic site open to the public.

Meanwhile, the U.S. Army's facility (originally known as the Columbia Barracks), which was built up the hill from the Fort Vancouver site, was renamed the Vancouver Barracks in 1879. It served as the headquarters of the Army's Department of the Columbia, a military subdivision that included all of Washington, Oregon, and Idaho.

Between 1849 and 1906, the army built 21 grand homes along what is now known as Officer's Row, on the northern boundary of the fort's agricultural area. Among the officers who once resided in the homes, which were considered among the "prettiest occupied by any military post in the United States," were future Civil War general Philip Sheridan, Brigadier General George C. Marshall, and a young Omar Bradley, who would later become a five-star general and the first chair of the Joint Chiefs of Staff.

The Marshall House on Fort Vancouver's Officers' Row was built in 1886 to serve as quarters for the post commander. It was named for Gen. George C. Marshall, who served as commander of the Vancouver Barracks from 1936 to 1938.

View of Fort Vancouver's three-story bastion, or blockhouse, a replica of the 1829 original, which had been constructed on that site in 1829.

The oldest of these homes, known as the Grant House, was built in 1849 and is named for Ulysses S. Grant, who served as the fort's Quartermaster between 1852 and 1853. Though he never lived in the house, it was named in his honor after he and his wife visited the post in 1879. Over the years, the Army also constructed a series of barracks, a Quartermaster's Depot, and other structures, many around a parade ground.

In the early 1920s, a former polo field adjacent to the barracks, which had been the site of a lumber mill that produced wood for airplanes during World War I, became one of the nation's first airfields. Known as Pearson Field after 1925, it was home to the 321st Observation Squadron, 96th Division from the mid-1920s until the 1940s.

The fort was designated a national monument in 1949 and later a national historic site. In 1996 the fort site was incorporated into the 366-acre Vancouver National Historic Reserve and, in 2007, was placed on the National Register of Historic Places.

21
Washington State School for the Blind

45.6308° N, 122.6476° W

On East 13th Street in Vancouver

From its earliest days as a territory, Washington sought to provide public educational facilities for those with disabilities. In 1886 the territorial legislature approved an order establishing a state school for the disabled, which had the unfortunate name "Washington State School for Defective Youth."

Within a few short years, the state had hired a director/teacher, a Presbyterian minister named W. D. McFarland, and acquired an abandoned boardinghouse in Vancouver to serve as a school. Just a year after the school was established, McFarland departed and was replaced as director by James Watson, who, with his wife, had experience teaching deaf students. Probably due to this, and despite its name, the modest two-story school largely catered to the hearing-impaired in its early years. In 1887 however, the school enrolled its first blind student.

Soon, recognizing that the school facilities were insufficient for teaching a growing student body (which, at the time, included students who were deaf, blind, and had a variety of intellectual disabilities), Watson, who strongly supported the idea of his students attending college, successfully petitioned the state government for increased funding. Between 1891 and 1905, the state allocated additional funds, which were used to purchase more land (the site would eventually grow to about 13 acres) and build new facilities.

Watson also realized that educating students with intellectual disabilities required different skills and facilities than those required for educating students who were deaf and blind. About 1892 those students were transferred to a school in Medical Lake, Washington. The Washington State School for the Deaf and Blind (the new name) operated until 1913, when it was split into two separate schools, both in Vancouver (the Washington School for the Deaf continues to operate in a separate facility about a mile away).

As part of this change, the state financed construction of a large, three-story, brick Administration Building for the School for the Blind. When completed in 1916, it housed not only offices but a gymnasium, a library, a dining hall, an auditorium, staff living quarters, and classrooms. During this time, the student population continued to grow, and additional buildings were added between 1912 and 1919, including boys' and girls' dormitories and an industrial-arts building. All of those structures (located at the southeast corner of the grounds) were built in the early 20th-century Classical Revival architectural style, with several designed by noted Washington architect Julius Zittel.

Additional facilities, including cottages, classrooms, a second auditorium, and a new gymnasium were added in more recent decades. Located about a block from Mill Plain Boulevard, one of Vancouver's major commercial

The three-story, Classical Revival-style Administration Building at the Washington School for the Blind was completed in 1916.

strips, the school is today surrounded by modest single-family homes. It offers classes for grades 6 to 12 and has about 50 enrolled students.

Four surviving structures constructed between 1912 and 1919, including the impressive Administration Building, and a Boiler Room building erected in 1885 were added to the National Register of Historic Places in 1993. Among the graduates of the school is famed jazz singer-pianist Diane Schuur, who attended from age 4 to 11 (then attended public school in her hometown of Tacoma). As of this writing, Schuur has released more than 26 albums and earned 2 Grammy Awards.

22
House of Providence
(PROVIDENCE ACADEMY)

45.6294° N, 122.6683° W

On East Evergreen Boulevard in downtown Vancouver

Half-hidden behind a handful of mature trees in downtown Vancouver, adjacent to Interstate 5 and across the street from the gleaming glass-and-metal city library, is an elegant, three-story, Colonial/Georgian Revival-style, red brick building that doesn't seem to belong amid the modern apartments and office buildings that surround it. Known as Providence Academy or House of Providence, it is one of Vancouver's oldest buildings, having been constructed between 1873 and 1874. It was conceived and designed by Mother Joseph Pariseau of the Sisters of Providence (also known as Mother Joseph of the Sacred Heart), a prominent figure in early Washington.

Pariseau was born Esther Pariseau in the Canadian province of Quebec in 1823. The daughter of a French-Canadian carriagemaker, she learned from her father about carpentry and woodworking. She also gained a knowledge of how to plan and build structures, which later gave her the nickname "The Builder."

When she was 20, Pariseau entered the Catholic order the Sisters of Charity of Providence in Montreal. Thirteen years later, she was selected to lead a group of five missionaries sent to the Pacific Northwest to establish schools, hospitals, and other facilities in the region. Because of her expertise in construction, she was an ideal choice; during her lifetime (she died in 1902), she served as the architect and construction manager of 11 hospitals, 7 academies, 5 Indian schools, and 2 orphanages in Washington, Oregon, Idaho, and Montana.

One of her more significant projects was Vancouver's Providence Academy, which originally served as boarding school, orphanage, and headquarters for the Sisters of Charity order. At the time it was built, it overlooked the growing town of Vancouver and was adjacent to the U.S. Army post at Fort Vancouver.

The academy remains an impressive and imposing structure. The oldest portion, the center buildings, originally formed a cruciform, with one wing reserved for boarders and day students, another for orphan girls, and another for orphan boys. In the center of the complex, on its second floor, was a two-and-a-half story Gothic-style chapel. In 1891 a large west wing, which included an auditorium, was added.

On the property grounds (the site encompasses seven acres), the sisters planted orchards and gardens with walkways. Over the years, several outbuildings were constructed on the site, including a barn, a stone root cellar, a convent and schoolhouse (later converted into a print shop), a laundry building, a power plant building, and an octagonal well house. In the 1930s, a kindergarten and gymnasium building was erected on the site.

In the 1950s, however, the demand for the services provided by the academy declined, particularly with the development of local parish schools. After several years serving as a girls academy, the facility was shuttered in 1966. For the next three years, the buildings stood empty and largely forgotten, home only to pigeons and trespassers. When the Sisters of

The House of Providence, also known as Providence Academy, was built between 1873 and 1874 to serve as a boarding school, orphanage, and headquarters for the Sisters of Charity order.

Charity seriously considered demolishing the main academy building, at that point the only structure still standing, descendants of Lowell Hidden, owner of the brick company that originally provided the materials to build the academy more than a century before, purchased it from the order. The family began slowly refurbishing the building, adding shops and offices, a Montessori School, and a restaurant. In 1978 it was added to the National Register of Historic Places.

In 2015 the building was acquired by the National Trust (formerly known as the Fort Vancouver National Trust), which replaced the roof, restored the chapel, and rehabilitated other parts of the structure. The new owner also added updated kitchen facilities for catered events and new audio-visual systems for presentations, as well as a modern HVAC system. The trust continues to explore other options as well, including converting part of the academy into a museum. The facility is open for public tours.

23
Covington House

45.6524° N, 122.6665° W

On East Evergreen Boulevard in downtown Vancouver

It's said that when Ulysses S. Grant was the quartermaster at the Vancouver Barracks, he was a frequent visitor to the nearby Covington House. During his 18 months at Fort Vancouver, during 1852 and 1853, Grant is believed to have ridden by horse to the home for social events and to enjoy musical recitals.

The house—really a large log cabin—was built in 1848 by Richard and Charlotte "Anna" Covington and is the oldest domestic home in Clark County. The Covingtons, who were from England, had been hired by the Hudson's Bay Company to serve as teachers for the children living at Fort Vancouver. From 1846 to 1848, they taught children at the fort. After that, however, they filed a land claim on 640 acres located in what became known as the Fourth Plain, or Orchards area, about seven to eight miles from the fort. There they built a large cabin of planed logs held together by mortise and tenon corners. The structure was designed to serve as both a boarding school and residence.

The cabin had a large cobblestone fireplace and chimney, and a loft where the children slept. The rest of the house served as a combined classroom, kitchen, dining room, and workroom. Adding to the rustic nature of its appearance, the structure had a simple gable roof with cedar shakes.

When Richard and Anna moved here, they brought along a piano—the first in the Pacific Northwest—as well as a guitar and a violin. Both were accomplished musicians who loved to play, and their home became one of the social centers of the community.

Shortly after arriving, Richard was assigned to also serve as one of the first justices of the peace for Clark County. A year later, he was elected county clerk under the Oregon Territory's Provisional Government, and in 1863 he served as justice of the peace again. In 1862 and again in 1863, Richard was also elected Clark County's school superintendent. In 1867 he was appointed to a position in the U.S. Patent Office. The new post required the Covingtons to relocate to Washington D.C., so they closed the school and sold the cabin and surrounding farm to William C. Hazard, who continued to operate it as a farm.

By the early 20th century, the log cabin, now owned by Fred Lockley, an executive with the *Oregon Journal*, was in disrepair, having been used for a time as an animal shelter. In 1925 members of the Vancouver business community, concerned about losing such an iconic part of the community's past, came together to raise funds to save and rehabilitate the building. The following year, Lockley donated the cabin to the city of Vancouver, with the proviso that it be relocated to a park setting.

After a community fundraising effort, the cabin was disassembled and reassembled on a site in Vancouver's Leverich Park that same year. A log lean-to was erected adjacent to the cabin. It contained a kitchen and other facilities that permitted it to be used as a venue for events.

The cabin was placed on the National Register of Historic Places in 1972. It continues to be owned and maintained by the city of Vancouver on land owned by the local school district and is currently operated by the Covington House Heritage Society as an event venue. It is open by appointment.

Built in 1848, Vancouver's Covington House, a large log-cabin-type structure, is the oldest domestic home in Clark County. It originally was used as a boardinghouse and school for the children of Hudson's Bay Company employees.

24
Cedar Creek Grist Mill

45.9384° N, 122.5834° W

On Northeast Grist Mill Road, 9 Miles East of Woodland

The Cedar Creek Grist Mill is the only Washington historical site that caters to bakers. That's because the mill, which was built in 1876, remains a working facility that produces flour, which visitors can purchase for making pancakes, scones, beer bread, or shortcakes. In fact, the mill's webpage offers recipes for all those delicacies and more.

Described as a "working museum," the mill offers tours of the inner workings of the historic gristmill, showing how it still operates today using water power and milling stones. In addition to its unique status as the only gristmill that has maintained its original structural integrity, Cedar Creek is set in a location right out of a fairy tale or a Thomas Kinkade painting. Surrounded by tall, moss-covered trees, the wooden mill, which sits on the banks of Cedar Creek, is without a doubt one of Washington's most picturesque historic sites.

The mill, located nine miles east of the town of Woodland, was erected by George W. Woodham and his sons, using wood supplied by A.C. Reid, who owned a sawmill about a mile downstream from the gristmill site. Woodham, an itinerant miller, was born in Illinois in 1827. He and his family settled north of Fort Vancouver in the mid-1870s and built a gristmill on Cedar Creek, which had a good year-round water flow. It was originally known as the Red Bird Mill.

Within a short time, farmers throughout the region were bringing their grain to the mill to be ground into flour, cornmeal, or livestock feed. Shortly after completing the mill, which boasted a large wooden water wheel, Woodham built a dam to form a millpond that fed into a flume that supplied water to the mill. Unfortunately, during the mill's first winter, the dam was damaged by debris carried in the swift-flowing creek. Faced with expensive repairs, in 1879 Woodham decided to sell the facility and relocate to Centralia with his equipment.

The mill's next owner, Mike Lynch, did not initially use the property. In 1888 he leased it to Gustave Utter. Utter replaced the wooden water wheel with a Leffel turbine, built a new flume, and constructed a log dam about 80 feet upstream. Utter tried his best to make the mill a profitable concern, trading out mill services for shares of grain and supplementing his income by hosting dances and musical entertainment and raising hogs, but in 1901 he realized he couldn't make it work and decided to sell.

The next owner was Gorund Roslund, who bought the mill in 1905 and got it operating again in 1909. Roslund added a shingle mill and, with his son Victor, opened a machine shop in the lower level of the mill (Victor also lived in the mill building). Later, another of Gorund's sons, Elmer, added a blacksmith shop and converted the upper floor into living space.

In the late 1950s, the Roslund family sold the mill to the Washington State Fisheries Department, which removed the old dam and built a fish ladder. In 1961 the Fort Vancouver Historical Society leased the mill, which had been neglected for many years, and replaced the original foundation. The society also helped get the mill placed on the National Register of Historic Places in 1975.

In 1980 the mill, still in need of repairs, was taken over by a local nonprofit organization, Friends of the Cedar Creek Grist Mill. Volunteers from the group replaced rotting posts and beams using traditional broad axes and adzes (a tool with

Despite its age, the Cedar Creek Grist Mill, constructed in 1876, continues be operational, using water power and milling stones to make flour. —Photo by Hank Moreno

an arched blade) to duplicate the original pieces. The flume was extended 650 feet into the creek to get water into the mill without having to rebuild the dam. On November 11, 1989, the Friends successfully began to grind wheat again in the old mill.

On the original mill site there apparently was a covered bridge adjacent to the property, which had been replaced by a truss bridge in 1935. The latter was unable to accommodate heavy vehicles, so in 1994 a new (and more picturesque) covered bridge was erected over the creek.

Today, the mill is open from 1 p.m. to 4 p.m. for tours on Saturdays, and sacks of milled flour are, of course, available for sale.

25
Grays River Covered Bridge

46.3543° N, 123.5815° W

Approximately 1.5 miles east of the town of Grays River

The Grays River Covered Bridge was originally built to help local dairy farmers get their milk across the river to the steamboats docked on the other side. According to Washington historian Kit Oldham, prior to the construction of the Grays River Bridge, only small footbridges spanned the river in the area. Horse carriages and farm wagons were able to cross the river only at low tide (because Grays River flows into the Columbia River, it experiences the tidal action of the Columbia River). Additionally, the steamboats that plied Grays River and connected the area to other regions were only able to dock on the river's northwest bank, while the farmers' lands were on the southeast side of the river.

In 1905 Hans P. Ahlberg, whose dairy farm was intersected by the river, persuaded Wahkiakum County officials to give him permission to build the wooden bridge at a cost of $2,700. When completed that year, the one-lane bridge measured about 155 feet long and 14 feet wide—wide enough to accommodate typical horse carriages and farm wagons. Timber for the original bridge came from local forests. Oldham noted that construction was largely done by local residents, with their labor counting toward their local tax assessments. He said this was a common trade-off in the early 1900s.

While initially the bridge was not covered, in 1908 a shell made of cedar boards with a capped tin roof was built around the bridge in order to protect the expensive wooden trusses from the often-rainy local weather. Rain also often caused the bridge planks to become too slick for livestock with metal shoes to safely cross. Several years after the cover was built, cables were attached to the structure to prevent it from being damaged by high winds. In 1915 protective cedar porches, or overhangs, were constructed over the two entrances to the bridge.

In the 1940s, a concrete support was placed on the upstream side of the center pier, along with other barriers, to divert floating logs and other debris from slamming into and damaging the bridge's supports. Later modifications included replacing the tin roof with a corrugated metal one in the mid-70s and constructing a new center pier in 1987, after the old one was damaged in a flood.

In 1971 the covered bridge was placed on the National Register of Historic Places, and by the 1980s, it had become a popular tourist attraction. An inspection of the bridge in 1987 indicated the presence of severe dry rot and other issues. In response, the load limit was seriously reduced (it was originally five tons), meaning it was no longer able to be used by farm trucks and other heavy equipment.

About a year later, Wahkiakum County officials decided to rehabilitate the bridge rather than replace it with something more contemporary. It committed nearly $300,000 to reconstruct the bridge using a steel truss (replacing the original wooden one) so that it met modern road-safety standards (it now has a 15-ton capacity). Construction crews salvaged as much of the original cedar siding as they could and incorporated it into the rehabilitated bridge, helping it retain as much of its original appearance as possible.

The project was completed in late September 1989, with the venerable bridge commemorated at a formal rededication ceremony.

The Grays River Covered Bridge is one of only a handful of covered bridges still in use in Washington.

26
St. Helens Hotel

46.3950° N, 122.5854° W

On North Market Boulevard in Chehalis

In the small town of Chehalis, the former St. Helens Hotel (now known as the St. Helens Apartments) truly stands out. Not only is it the tallest building in town at six stories, but with its unusual wedge design, it is also the community's most distinctive structure and is prominently featured in the city's official logo.

The building can trace its roots to the early 1890s, when the first St. Helens Hotel was built on the site. This was a three-story wooden structure, constructed between 1890 and 1894 by the Chehalis Land and Timber Company, a prominent local company that promoted the town's development. Part of the impetus for the Chehalis Land and Timber Company to build the hotel there was its active effort to shift the commercial center of the community from Main Street to its holdings on Northern Market Boulevard. The original hotel was designed by a Tacoma architectural firm, Bullard & Bullard, which was also responsible for the Provident Building and the Washington State History Research Center, both in Tacoma. Chehalis Land and Timber sold the hotel in the 1890s to William West, who had been managing the property. In 1904, West's son, William Francis West, took over management of the hotel, eventually inheriting it following his father's death in 1915.

From the time it opened, the St. Helens was a popular place for travelers and visitors. In fact, in May 1914, former President Theodore Roosevelt stayed at the hotel. In 1917 William Francis West decided to build a new, larger, more modern structure on the site. Rather than demolish the original hotel, he removed a tower and the front porch and sold the structure, which was relocated to a site three blocks north. There it was converted into the Strickland Apartments, which remained in use until it was condemned following a fire in 1978. The ruins were demolished in 1982.

The new St. Helens was a far grander, Neoclassical structure that was built in stages between 1917 and 1921. Designed by architect Charles E. Troutman of Aberdeen, Washington, the hotel offered 150 guest rooms at the time of its opening. It is also an example of what architectural historians call a two-part commercial space. The ground floor is occupied by retail shops while the upper floors contain the accommodations.

Like the original wooden hotel, the new version was essentially a triangular-shaped structure, built in that way because of the irregular shape of the lot. It has an imposing, multistory gray brick façade that extends half a block on Market Street in Chehalis' downtown district. One unusual aspect of the hotel's long history is that it was associated with a single family, the Wests, for more than 80 years.

According to its National Register of Historic Places Nomination, the hotel was managed in its early years by John Abbe, who arrived in Chehalis with his brother-in-law, William West, in the 1860s. After West's son, William Francis West, acquired ownership of the hotel, he constructed the new, larger St. Helens. The younger West continued to be the principal owner until his death in 1963.

After William Francis West's death, his widow placed ownership of the hotel with the William F. West Foundation, which supported local philanthropic efforts such as scholarships for college-bound Chehalis students. In 1976 the foundation sold the hotel, which had experienced a business downturn after

With its triangular shape, the six-story St. Helens Hotel (now known as the St. Helens Apartments) has long been a landmark in the community of Chehalis.

construction of Interstate 5 removed much of the traffic from downtown. The new owners closed the hotel and began the process of converting the building into apartments, which opened under a new name, the St. Helens Inn.

According to the *Chehalis Daily Chronicle*, over the next few years the property began to decline until it was purchased in 2005 by a Bellingham-based property-management company, Daylight Properties, which specialized in rehabilitating and repurposing historic properties. The company spent more than $1 million on renovations and upgrades on the property, which had been added to the National Register of Historic Places in 1991. Currently called the St. Helens Apartments, the former hotel has 54 residential units including 8 studios, 34 one-bedroom apartments, and 12 two-bedroom units. The ground floor continues to serve as retail space for 7 businesses.

27
Claquato Church

46.643° N, 123.022° W

On Water Street, 7 Miles West of Chehalis

The tower on Washington's oldest church is topped not with a cross, like most other Christian houses of worship, but with a crown of thorns. Not real thorns, but jagged pieces of wood that symbolize the prickly wreath that, according to the Bible, was placed on Jesus' head during his crucifixion.

Called the Claquato Church (Claquato was the settlement where the church still stands), its look is unique among Washington churches, not only for its crown of thorns, but also because it resembles the meeting houses more commonly found in the Puritan settlements of New England. While architectural historians aren't certain the design was intentional, they acknowledge that many of the area's settlers originally came from the eastern U.S., so it may have provided them with a measure of familiarity in a brand-new place.

The tiny, one-and-a-half-story wooden church—the building is a mere 20-by-30 feet square and can only accommodate about 30 people—sits in the enclave of Claquato, located three miles west of Chehalis. Erected in 1858, it originally served the local Methodist congregation. It is one of only two churches built during Washington's territorial era that remain standing (the other is the Episcopalian Church in Port Townsend, built in 1865).

The Claquato Church was built on land owned by Lewis H. Davis, the first white settler in the Claquato area. Davis, along with his brother-in-law, J. D. Clinger, apparently oversaw its construction. Davis's just-completed sawmill supplied the lumber, a local blacksmith forged the nails, and Clinger made the doors and casings. Pews, a pulpit, and a pastor's chair were donated by parishioners from the nearby settlement of Boistfort. To put an accent on the New England vibe of the place, the bronze bell that hangs in the belfry was cast in Boston and transported by ship via Cape Horn.

Davis was an important figure in the region's history because he not only built the first home in Claquato, but he also embarked on an ambitious road-building effort to link communities north of the Columbia River to the port settlements of Olympia and Fort Steilacoom. In getting the road constructed, Davis worked closely with the U.S. Army, which provided much of the funding. Thus this north-south artery became known as Military Road (it still exists today).

Largely as a result of the road, Claquato became an important stop for travelers, especially after Olympia was named territorial capital. In the 1860s, Claquato boasted two hotels, a general store, stables, a blacksmith shop, the church (which also served as a school for a short time), and several other businesses. In the early 1870s, however, construction of the Northern Pacific Railway to the east of Claquato started the beginning of the community's decline. In 1873 the railroad established the town of Chehalis, which soon eclipsed Claquato in importance.

Regular services were held in the Claquato Church until the mid-1930s, when the church was closed due to a lack of members. Over the next several years, the building stood vacant and was subject to vandalism. Then, in the early 1950s, Lewis County assumed ownership of the abandoned church and gave permission to the local American Legion Post 22 to restore the structure as a public service. The renovated Claquato Church was completed in August 1953 and rededicated as a memorial to the pioneers of Lewis County. It was placed on the National Register of Historic Places in 1973. Today, about 100 people live in Claquato, which is generally considered part of the greater Centralia-Chehalis area.

This tiny wooden church in the settlement of Claquato, built in 1858, is the oldest house of worship in the state of Washington.

28
Cape Disappointment Historic District

46.2758° N, 124.0521° W

On Cape Disappointment Trail, 7 miles south of Ilwaco

Located on the cliffs above the northern part of the mouth of the Columbia River, the Cape Disappointment Lighthouse was constructed in 1854 to help keep ships from wrecking on the cape's rocky shores. The cape, which is an outcropping that juts into the river near the Washington-Oregon border, gained its descriptive name in 1788, when a British trader named John Meares, who was searching for the mouth of the Columbia River, actually found what he was seeking but couldn't continue because of the presence of dangerous sandbars (he believed he had only discovered a bay). Frustrated that he had not been able to sail into the river, he named the headlands Cape Disappointment.

Prior to that, Spanish explorer Bruno Heceta, who also mistakenly believed the inlet adjacent to the cape was a bay, had named it "Bahia de La Asuncion" or "Bay of the Assumption." Like Meares, he did not come ashore at the cape, but viewed it from his ship.

The first non-natives to set foot on the cape were members of the Lewis and Clark expedition, who, in November 1805, camped there. Most historians believe that the expedition's arrival at the cape marked the moment when it actually reached the Pacific Ocean, which was part of its mandate. A few years later, in 1818, the *Ontario*, a sloop-of-war flying the flag of the new American government, arrived in the area to claim it as part of the United States. A crew from the ship nailed a leaden tablet to a tree to mark their claim.

In subsequent years, ship traffic to the area increased enormously due to the development of a thriving fur trade in the Pacific Northwest. In 1841 the United States Exploring Expedition, led by Lt. Charles Wilkes, visited the area and proposed that a small fort be established at the cape to secure the area (as well as the Columbia River) for the U.S., keeping it out of the hands of any foreign interests.

This suggestion alarmed the British-owned Hudson's Bay Company, which still had considerable financial interests in the region, and in 1845, the company purchased the cape. That ownership, however, was short-lived, as all of the territory south of the 49th parallel was transferred to the United States by Britain as a result of the Oregon Treaty of 1846.

Six years later, a presidential order established that all of Cape Disappointment was to become part of a military complex. The following year, the government decided to build a lighthouse on the cape to warn ships about the Columbia River's entrance, particularly the presence of the Columbia Bar, a shifting sandbar that was known as "the graveyard of ships."

While the first ship transporting materials to build the light tower, the *Oriole*, ran aground near the cape (resulting in the loss of all materials and the ship), a second vessel was able to bring the shipment in intact. Construction of the tower began in 1854, but the project wasn't completed until 1856, when the lighthouse lens was finally installed.

The finished lighthouse, made of brick covered with stucco, measured 53 feet high and stood 220 feet above sea level, providing a light that could be seen 24 miles out to sea. To accommodate the massive 8-foot-tall, 6-foot-wide, 6-ton lens, which was lighted using oil as fuel, the rooms and living spaces for the lighthouse keeper were constructed adjacent to the tower rather than inside.

In 1898 the original lens was relocated to the nearby North Head Lighthouse, which had been built that year when it became obvious that the Cape Disappointment Lighthouse could not be seen very well by ships traveling from the north. The Cape Disappointment Lighthouse soon received a replacement lens, which was not electrified until 1937.

The lighthouse operations, which are overseen by the U.S. Coast Guard, were automated in 1973 and it remains in use as a beacon for seafaring traffic. In 1975, as part of Cape Disappointment Historic District in Cape Disappointment State Park, the lighthouse complex was added to the National Register of Historic Places. The complex, however, hasn't been renovated or repainted for several years due to Coast Guard budget constraints.

Perched on the cliffs above the point where the Columbia River meets the Pacific Ocean, the Cape Disappointment Lighthouse, erected in 1855, is the oldest lighthouse in Washington state. –Photo by Hank Moreno

Scenic overlook of the Columbia River above Vantage Bridge (east of Ellensburg). The Columbia bends west, south, and east through central Washington before forming the border between Washington and Oregon then flowing into the Pacific Ocean.

CENTRAL

Geology helps define a place, which is certainly true in the center part of Washington, which contains some of the state's most striking natural attractions. It includes places like Dry Falls, an Ice Age remnant that was once the world's largest waterfall at more than 400 feet, or the Drumheller Channel Basalt Columns, a series of 50-foot-high, hexagonal stone pillars formed over millions of years by cooling and contracting lava.

Because of the region's rich geological past, as well as more recent manmade developments such as the massive Grand Coulee Dam, central Washington is a land with vast and productive agricultural lands. Many communities in this middle part of the state owe their existences to the things that are grown here, such as hay, wheat, apples, wine grapes, hops, and other crops.

While towns in the center and southern part of this region owe a major debt to the successful development of agriculture, in the northwestern, mountainous portion of this section of Washington mining for coal and precious minerals like gold and silver led to the creation and early growth of communities like Liberty, Roslyn, and Cle Elum. Later, the development of Hanford and the Tri-Cities area (Richland, Pasco, and Kennewick) was due to the U.S. government, which invested millions there to tame the atom.

This part of Washington also encompasses the 1.13-million-acre Yakama Nation, a sovereign nation recognized by the federal government and managed by the Bureau of Indian Affairs. This reservation, located on the east side of the Cascade Mountains and including part of Mount Adams, was established in 1855 by a treaty between Washington Territorial Governor Isaac Stevens and tribal representatives.

Some of the tribal leaders did not believe those representatives had the authority to cede traditional tribal lands to the Washington Territory (which had been created in 1853). This disagreement, and other injustices committed against tribal members, led to the Yakima War of 1855–1858. After hostilities ceased, members of various regional tribes, which included the Klikitat, Palus, Walla Walla, Wanapam, Wenatchi, Wishram, and Yakama people, were placed (sometimes against their will) on the Yakama reservation, which included the Fort Simcoe Indian School. Today at Fort Simcoe Historical State Park, located on the reservation, visitors can explore much of this sad history.

29
Liberty Ghost Town

47.2537° N, 120.6689° W

28 miles north of Ellensburg via WA State Route 97

People usually associate Washington with industries like timber, fishing, or hydroelectric power. But more than a century and a half ago, a tiny enclave in the north-central part of the state came into being because of something else—gold. That place, which eventually became known as Liberty, was established in 1873 as the Swauk Mining District. The name derived from its location on Williams Creek near its confluence with Swauk Creek (Swauk is an anglicized version of a Kittitas word meaning "deep").

Gold was discovered in the region in 1868 by novice miners who were traveling on a Native American trail that passed through the area, located about 28 miles north of Ellensburg. The group camped for lunch and one of its members, Benton Goodwin, decided to do some panning for gold in an adjacent creek. Goodwin uncovered several small golden nuggets, which other members of his party insisted were nothing more than "fool's gold" or iron pyrite. Eventually, they packed up to continue on their way, but not before naming the place, with tongue in cheek, Discovery Bar.

Five years later, however, Goodwin and his brother, Newton, joined by three others, decided to take another look at Discovery Bar. During this second visit, the party found small gold flakes as well as gold nuggets. While the five initially tried to keep their discovery secret, word soon spread and within a short time, hundreds of prospectors had descended on the small valley to pan and mine for gold.

During the next several decades, the Swauk Mining District saw several booms and busts, including a boom in 1891 that had the *Ellensburg Capital* newspaper describing the latest find as the "Mother Lode." The original camp was called Williams Creek until 1897, when it was renamed Meaghersville after Thomas F. Meagher, who, in addition to being one of the town's earliest merchants, is credited with finding the gold-bearing channel of Williams Creek. In 1892 the name was changed one final time to Liberty, when a post office was established in the town.

These days, about a dozen residents, many descended from pioneer settlers, continue to live and, in some cases, work in the area, hoping to make that one big find that many believe is yet to be discovered.

The 17-acre Liberty townsite, which was placed on the National Register of Historic Places in 1974, remains a quiet, quaint village consisting of about a dozen wooden structures built between the late 19th century and the early to mid-20th century. Many have been rebuilt or renovated over the years into private residences. In fact, Liberty is often referred to as a "living ghost town" because it has never been completely abandoned.

Among the most prominent buildings still standing in the town is a two-story hotel and boardinghouse, built in the 1890s. Constructed of rough-sawed lumber with a board and batten exterior, the structure was used as a hotel until the 1920s, when it was converted into a private residence. Similarly, the original grocery store and butcher shop, both also built in the 1890s, were transformed into homes in the early 20th century. Thomas Meagher's former cabin also remains standing (barely) beside Williams Creek.

Other surviving structures from the town's early days include a log cabin house, believed to have been built in the 1890s; the former stage and livery office, also built in the 1890s, which was used as a rock shop for many years; and several houses, which also date back to the 1890s and remain in use.

Visitors will also find a covered display containing a replica of a Virden arrastra, which was a crude mill for grinding and pulverizing gold ore. An arrastra like this one was used in the processing of gold ore found in the area. Interestingly, Liberty gold was found via both placer mining (e.g. flakes and nuggets removed from the creek) and hard-rock mining in the hills above the town, where crystallized gold was uncovered.

Reportedly, the largest nugget ever found in the state of Washington was a 22-ounce hunk discovered at Liberty in the 1880s. More recently, in 2013 a prospector using a metal detector on his private claim uncovered a 16.25-ounce nugget and a 13-ounce nugget, which had a combined worth of more than $55,000.

The tiny enclave of Liberty, today home to about a dozen residents, is a self-described "living ghost town." It traces its beginnings to the discovery of gold in the area in 1868.

30
Roslyn Historical Cemeteries

47.21980° N, 121.99770° W

3 miles southeast of downtown Roslyn on Memorial Road

In the tiny former mining town of Roslyn, the dead vastly outnumber the living. That becomes readily apparent when visiting the Roslyn Historic Cemeteries, a collection of 27 separate fraternal and public burial grounds spread over 15 acres and containing an estimated 5,000 graves that represent at least 24 nationalities.

Tucked into the eastern slopes of the Cascade Mountains, about four miles northwest of Cle Elum, the community of Roslyn, which today boasts a population of about 950 souls, traces its beginning to 1883, when prospectors and a few homesteaders began to settle in the area known as Lake Cle Elum country. Interestingly, the early miners knew of the presence of large quantities of coal in the area but generally ignored the black rock because they were searching for gold and silver.

That changed sometime in 1883, when Nez "Cayuse" Jensen filed a claim on 160 acres in what is now downtown Roslyn and built a one-room cabin on his land (a reconstruction of the cabin stands at 200 W. Utah Avenue in Roslyn). Jensen and a neighbor, John Stone, began mining coal with a pick and shovel, and then transported it via pony and buckboard to blacksmith shops in nearby Ellensburg.

In May 1886, prospectors from the Northern Pacific Railway, who were searching for new sources of coal, uncovered and claimed large seams in the Roslyn area. In August, the railroad sent a small team of workers to mine the coal and quickly built a spur to move the product down to the main line at Cle Elum. Word soon spread that the railroad was mining coal in Roslyn, and within a few weeks, hundreds of workers were on site.

Supervising the workers was Logan M. Bullitt, vice president of the Northern Pacific Coal Company. Bullitt is credited with naming Roslyn, though accounts vary as to why he chose that name. According to one, Bullitt named it after the Delaware hometown of a "vivacious maiden" with whom he had fallen in love. Another version is that he named it after the Long Island town in which a good friend, poet and editor William Cullen Bryant, lived.

In September 1886, the railroad laid out the townsite of Roslyn. The first businesses to open in Roslyn included a general store and saloon, a hotel, a boardinghouse, livery stables, and a handful of other commercial services. By 1888 Roslyn boasted more than 1,000 residents. In June of that year, however, a fire broke out in the business district, destroying nearly every building. The merchants quickly rebuilt, this time using brick instead of wood.

About a year after Roslyn was founded, the railroad donated land just outside town for a small cemetery. Over time, it was expanded by a variety of ethnic and fraternal organizations. Sadly, because mining is such dangerous work, Roslyn's cemeteries were periodically busy. On May 10, 1892, for example, an explosion in one of the mines killed 45 miners. Apparently, gases and extremely flammable coal dust ignited when miners were attempting to connect an airway to a deeper level in the mine. The tragedy was the deadliest coal-mine disaster in the history of Washington state. Additionally, Roslyn experienced a deadly typhoid epidemic in 1890, as well as a diphtheria outbreak in 1896 and a smallpox epidemic in 1900.

In the late 19th and early 20th centuries, the town of Roslyn was a thriving coal-mining center that attracted workers from all over the world. Due to the dangerous nature of mining, the town has an impressive 27 fraternal and public cemeteries spread over 15 acres and containing more than 5,000 graves representing at least 24 nationalities.

One of Roslyn's defining characteristics was its racial and ethnic diversity. The coal mines attracted workers from all over the world. By 1900 an estimated 40 percent of the population was foreign born, including large numbers of people from Croatia, England, Germany, Scotland, Wales, Poland, Italy, Lithuania, Slovenia, and Serbia.

The community also had a large black population—about 22 percent in 1900. In 1888 Roslyn coal miners went on strike, and the mining company brought in African American workers from the Midwest and East to break it. The dispute was eventually settled, but many of the black miners stayed on. Historians believe tensions between whites and blacks never reached a boiling point because there was plenty of work to go around.

This melting-pot population is well represented in Roslyn's various individual cemeteries. These include Moose, Eagles, Redmen, Masonic, Odd Fellows, and the New and Old Knights of Pythias cemeteries for members of those organizations, and the Silvio Pellico, Druid, and Cacciatori D'Africa cemeteries for members of various Italian organizations. The complex also saw the development of Polish, Slovakian, Serbian, Croatian, Sokol (Czech), and Mt. Olivet (African American) cemeteries. This unusual diversity, in fact, played an important role in the cemeteries (along with the town of Roslyn) being placed on the National Register of Historic Places in 1978.

31
Wells House

47.4313° N, 120.3336° W

On Nelson Avenue in West Wenatchee, adjacent to Wenatchee Valley College

The drive to the historic Wells House takes you through a neat and modest residential part of the city of Wenatchee—leading you to wonder if you're heading the right way. Known as the "Cobblestone Castle," because of its massive exterior stone turret, the Wells House doesn't fit in with the surrounding neighborhood.

But the home's environs weren't always the way they appear today. At the time of its construction, the Wells House was surrounded by fruit orchards and not homes. In fact, when it was completed in 1909, atop a knoll that offered a commanding view of the Wenatchee Valley, it was considered to be the finest country home ever constructed in Washington state. Since then, however, the city of Wenatchee has grown up and around the majestic home. In addition to being encircled by single-family residences, the Wells House sits adjacent to Wenatchee Valley College.

The massive mansion on the hill remains an impressive edifice, and it was certainly an appropriate residence for its original owners, William and Adelaide Clark. W. T. Clark, as he was usually known, is considered the father of the Wenatchee Valley because he developed the Highline Canal, which brought water into the valley and helped to transform the area into the "Apple Capital of the World."

Clark was a land developer who initially became wealthy developing irrigation projects in the Yakima Valley. In 1902 he and a partner, Marvin Chase, relocated to Wenatchee and established the Wenatchee Canal Company. One of the company's projects was the 34-mile Highline Canal Project, which transported water from the Wenatchee River to East Wenatchee through a series of gravity-fed flumes and pipes.

Clark's investments, which also included apple orchards, made him wealthy, and in time he and his wife decided to construct a 10-room, Craftsman-style home on a hill overlooking the growing community. Adelaide, who designed the house, had construction crews utilize local materials such as river rock from the Columbia River. She also designed unique apple-patterned stained-glass windows for the home.

When completed, the structure was three stories tall with a full basement. The walls of the basement and the first floor are constructed of native square-cut rock, which is more than a foot thick. The upper floors are of a wood-frame construction and covered with cedar shingles. The home also boasts a large tower, or turret, made of native rock that extends from the ground floor to the uppermost height of the house. With its crenulated battlement, the tower definitely resembles that of a medieval castle.

In 1919 the Clarks, who by then had suffered financial reversals, decided to sell their home to another pioneer Wenatchee family, A. Z. and Emogene Wells. The Wellses had arrived in Wenatchee in 1902. Soon after, A. Z. Wells and his nephew, Alfred Morris, opened a successful hardware store. Over the next few years, Wells expanded his ventures to include growing, packing, and selling fruit. By the time he died in 1950, his hardware business was reportedly the largest in north-central Washington and he owned more than 900 acres of fruit orchards.

A. Z. and Emogene, who had no children, resided in the home that now bears their name for more than thirty years. In

1949 they established a charitable foundation to benefit the Wenatchee area. One of their bequests was to the Wenatchee School District, to which they left the house and surrounding five acres for use as the location of Wenatchee Valley College, which was just being established.

From the 1950s to the early 1970s, the house was used as a classroom, for campus housing, and for administrative offices, but little money was spent on maintenance, and it was eventually abandoned. After sitting vacant for several years, the building fell into serious disrepair, with the turret starting to separate from the main structure. In the mid-1970s, when the college revealed it was considering demolishing the house, a group formed to save the historic structure, which had been placed on the National Register of Historic Places in 1973—the first house placed on the National Register in Washington state. Called the Wells House Committee, the group, aided by the Wenatchee Valley College and the Wenatchee Valley Museum, spent several decades raising funds to renovate and restore the house.

By 2017 a substantial portion of the work had been completed, and the house and its neatly groomed grounds were reopened for public tours and to host special events.

Constructed in 1909 by William T. Clark, one of Wenatchee's founders, this impressive three-story house with turret, which boasts a stone exterior made using Columbia River rock, sits on a hill overlooking the city.

32
Leavenworth Ski Hill Historic District

47.6141° N, 120.6687° W

At the Intersection of Ski Hill Drive and Titus Road in Leavenworth

On five occasions in the 20th century, America's best ski jumpers made their way to the small town of Leavenworth, Washington, to see who could fly the farthest. They came here because a ski area just outside of town, known as Ski Hill, boasted one of the largest ski-jump ramps in the country. Ski Hill, in fact, hosted the U.S. ski-jump championships in 1941, 1959, 1967, 1974, and 1978. Perhaps the best-known jumper to come out of Leavenworth was Ron Steele, who was the highest placed American jumper in the 1972 Olympics in Sapporo, Japan.

Ski Hill's story began when the Leavenworth Winter Sports Club (LWSC) was founded in 1928. Committed to developing facilities and activities that promoted skiing, the club partnered with the U.S. Forest Service to build a ski jump for local competitions on the eastern slope of Tumwater Mountain. The club continues to operate Ski Hill's facilities under a lease with the U.S. Forest Service.

In its early years, the LWSC hosted an annual ski-jump competition in the area, starting in 1929. As a result of the success of the inaugural event, in 1930 the club received a special-use permit from the Forest Service to build and maintain two ski jumps, two toboggan runs, a parking area, and a clubhouse. In 1936 the site was greatly expanded with the construction of the ski lodge and other facilities by workers from the Civilian Conservation Corps (CCC). The workers' camp was called Camp Icicle, which operated within the Wenatchee National Forest.

The two-and-a-half-story lodge, a key component of the 17-acre historic district, was constructed in a rustic style using logs, with a concrete and stone foundation. It also has a large stone chimney and basement. Much of the furniture inside the lodge, such as the wooden tables and benches, were hand built by the CCC. The lodge is still in use today.

The 90-meter ski jump was constructed in the early 1930s and rebuilt in 1957, after the original collapsed. The new ramp, now known as the Bakke Hill Ski Jump (after two pioneering local ski enthusiasts, Magnus and Hermod Bakke, who were instrumental in building the facilities), was erected on the site of the original ramp and featured a timber trestle and wooden decking. During the facility's mid-20th-century heyday as the host of national championship ski-jump competitions, Ski Hill attracted thousands of spectators, many of whom arrived on chartered trains from the Seattle area.

As a result of increased competition from newer and more challenging ski jump facilities in the country, the Bakke jump was closed in 1979, after hosting its last American ski-jump championship the previous winter. While listed as a major component of the historic district, the jump has not been used in decades and is slowly disintegrating.

Other structures listed as historically significant include a men's restroom, built in 1938 in a similar rustic style to match the lodge, and the garage/ticket booth structure, which was erected in 1940. The garage/ticket booth building remains in use while the men's room is closed to the public. The historic district also includes the contributing landscape, as the site's vegetation and topographical features were modified over the years to accommodate the ski area.

While the Bakke jump and other facilities are closed down, Ski Hill is still active. In 1970 a pair of smaller practice ski-jump terraces were added north of the lodge. While not considered historic, the newer jumps continue the site's historical role in training ski jumpers. Today, in addition to offering the 15- and 27-meter jumping hills, Ski Hill has a tubing hill, two rope tows, 8 kilometers of cross-country ski trails, and the historic lodge. The Leavenworth Ski Hill Historic District, located only 1.6 miles from the community's downtown, was added to the National Register of Historic Places in 2013.

The Leavenworth Ski Hill Historic District includes a two-and-a-half-story lodge and the remnants of a ski jump where Olympic skiers trained and competed in the mid-20th century.

33
Teapot Dome Service Station

46.4047° N, 120.2694° W

On 1st Avenue, off Exit 52 from I-82 E in Zillah

Jack Ainsworth wanted his new service station to grab the attention of passing motorists. Rather than simply rely on a big sign—although he had one of those—Ainsworth built his station to resemble a giant teapot.

The unusual design was his humorous response—said to have been concocted after a late-night drinking session with his buddies—to a headline-grabbing scandal that rocked the national political scene at that time. Known as the Teapot Dome Scandal, the affair involved the U.S. Secretary of the Interior, Albert B. Fall, who had secretly granted leases for drilling on valuable government oil reserves to two private companies in return for substantial bribes. One of the oil reserve sites was located in Teapot Dome, Wyoming (hence the name).

Investigators uncovered evidence that Fall had accepted $385,000 in illegal payments from the two oil companies. He was found guilty of the charges and served a year in prison—becoming the first former cabinet official ever sent to prison for misconduct in office.

So in 1922, at the height of the scandal, Ainsworth designed and built his one-of-a-kind Teapot service station on a lot adjacent to his father's general store. No doubt he understood the irony in peddling oil products from a structure designed to evoke an oil scandal that shook the nation.

The early 20th century was when the national highway system was being developed in the U.S. It wasn't unusual for roadside businesses, such as service stations, to seek to stand out. One of the ways to do that was to incorporate whimsical architecture into the design of the business. These structures, which became known as "follies," included a service station built to resemble an airplane in Tennessee and several Shell stations constructed in the shape of a clamshell in North Carolina.

Ainsworth's folly was a 13-foot-high, circular-frame building with a cone-shaped roof, a concrete spout, and a handle made of sheet metal. Resting on a concrete pad, the exterior was covered with wood shingles. Multi-paned windows on either side of the door provided light to the interior of the building. Originally located on U.S. Highway 410, between Zillah and Granger, the station boasted a small outhouse structure as well as several gas pumps and a tall pole atop which was a lit sign that read simply "Gas."

In 1928 Ainsworth sold the Teapot Dome Service Station to A. J. Thomas and his wife, Ruth, who continued to operate it as a family business until 1989. The Thomases made one significant change in 1978, when, during the construction of Interstate 82, they decided to relocate the station, which by then had become a beloved local landmark, to a site about 1.2 miles west on the old Yakima Valley Highway, which runs perpendicular to the interstate. In 1985 it was added to the National Register of Historic Places.

In 1989 the Thomases sold the property to Lyn Dasso, who operated it as a gas station until about 2006. That year, when Dasso closed the business, the building was purchased by the city of Zillah, which worked to raise funds to rehabilitate it. Six years later, it was relocated to a small park at the city's southwest entrance (at 116 First Avenue). The structure (including the outhouse) was restored to its original condition and converted into the city's visitors center.

These days, any motorist exiting Interstate 82 and driving into Zillah will find it impossible to miss the unusual landmark. After more than a century, it still garners the attention of passing motorists. No doubt, Jack Ainsworth would've been proud.

Created in an era when the architectural design of commercial buildings would sometimes serve as a promotional tool, Zillah's Teapot Dome Gas Station resembles a giant teapot.

34
Marble Ranch Round Barn

46.2422° N, 119.8946° W

At the intersection of Pleasant Road and Old Inland Empire Highway East, 1 mile south of Grandview

For a brief time in the late 19th and early 20th centuries, many progressive-minded farmers believed round barns were better than the traditional rectangular structures. It was thought that they were sturdier and more capable of handling severe weather, especially thunderstorms in the Midwest, and they permitted farmers to work around a central silo, which was thought to be more efficient.

As a result, between about 1880 and 1920, hundreds of round barns cropped up on farms throughout America, particularly in the Midwest. This fad even reached the Evergreen State, with about a dozen erected, mostly in the early 20th century. One of the oldest and best examples of this unusual style of barn architecture in Washington is the Marble Ranch Round Barn, also known as Cornell-Marble Round Barn, located near the intersection of Pleasant Road and Old Prosser Road in Grandview.

The two-story, circular wooden building, which has a circumference of 200 feet, was the brainchild of farmer Sylvester D. Cornell, who built it between 1912 and 1916. The barn boasts a 50-foot silo that rises above the round roof line, outwardly radiating interior rafters, exterior tongue-and-groove siding, 4 sliding wooden doors, and 16 fixed-sash windows.

Cornell not only operated a dairy farm, he also raised swine as well as record amounts of corn. In 1924, in fact, he harvested an amazing 21 tons, 740 pounds of corn on his farm, which, according to the November 9, 1924, edition of the *Tacoma Daily Ledger*, made him Washington's "champion ensilage grower."

Born in New York in 1888, Cornell came to the Grandview area around 1910. According to a story about him, that appeared in the *White Bluffs* [Washington] *Spokesman* on November 2, 1923, Cornell homesteaded his farm property in 1916.

"This field was sagebrush at the time," the newspaper reported. "A crop of turnips was grown on the field in 1916, followed by wheat as a nurse crop for alfalfa. Good crops of alfalfa were obtained each year. . . . In our opinion, Mr. Cornell's success in growing several crops is the result of good tillage, the keeping of dairy cows and hogs and the application of manure to this land."

In addition to the round barn, Cornell erected a one-and-a-half-story frame farmhouse, which is still standing. He also married and started a family. However, on August 28, 1925, Cornell tragically died at the age of 37. Following his death, his widow, Ada, sold the farm and moved to California with their young son, Lloyd.

By 1945 the property was in the hands of John H. Marble, who at one time was among the world's leading growers of irises (his catalog was distributed throughout the U.S.). After acquiring the farm, Marble planted much of the surrounding land in irises and utilized the round barn for storage. The Marble family continued to own the property until the late 20th century, when it was acquired by Sorenson Farms, which continues to use it.

Over the years, the barn has been well-maintained, receiving several state and federal grants to pay for roofing and other improvements. The property was listed on the National Register of Historic Places in 1987.

The Marble Ranch Round Barn, a.k.a. the Cornell-Marble Round Barn, is a good example of a style of barns that became popular in the country in the late 19th and early 20th centuries. Circular barns were thought to be sturdier and more efficient.

35
Fort Simcoe Historical State Park

46.3426° N, 120.8366° W

8 miles west of White Swan on Fort Simcoe Road

The natural beauty of Fort Simcoe State Park, with its tall oaks and beautifully restored historic buildings, stands in sharp contrast to the fort's problematic past. Built in August 1856, Fort Simcoe's original purpose was to keep watch on the native Yakama people. Later it served as an Indian boarding school tasked with assimilating Yakama children into the white American culture.

This complicated history, in fact, is what makes Fort Simcoe worthy of continued interest. Indeed, the Yakama Nation reservation, on which it is located, successfully petitioned the state in 2022 to begin the process of reinterpreting the 200-acre park site. "It [the Fort Simcoe area] was one of the main areas that we congregated and lived during certain times of the year," Arlen Washines, Yakama Nation Deputy Director for the Department of Human Services, said in a Northwest Public Broadcasting feature that year. "That's the story I told [to park officials] and that's the story the state parks manager wants to tell as well."

Prior to the fort's construction, the verdant site served as a traditional camping and resting place on a heavily traveled path used by the Yakama and other tribes to travel from the Yakima Valley (the tribe spells its name with an "a," while the city and valley spell it with an "i") to the tribe's traditional fishing areas on the Columbia River. It was an ideal location, with its groves of mature oak trees and the presence of a natural spring, known as *Mool-Mool*, or bubbling water. The fort's name, Simcoe, was derived from the Sahaptin word, *Sim-ku-ee*, meaning "saddle-like dip in a hill."

In the late 1840s, hostilities began breaking out between many of the Pacific Northwest tribes and white settlers, who were encroaching on tribal lands. Following the creation of the Washington Territory in March 1853, Isaac Stevens, governor of the new territory, forced the tribes into treaty negotiations that would have them sell the bulk of their lands and relocate to reservations. On June 9, 1855, representatives of the Yakama and 13 other tribes reluctantly signed the agreement, which became known as the Treaty with the Yakama. It ceded more than 12 million acres to the U.S. Government in return for $200,000, paid over a number of years. The treaty also specified the tribes would live on the smaller reservation land they were left with.

Stevens also pledged to the tribes that white miners and settlers would not trespass on these tribal lands before the treaty was ratified by the U.S. Senate. Unfortunately, it was a promise he could not keep, particularly after gold was discovered in the Colville, Washington, area, northeast of the Yakama reservation. That discovery brought a flood of miners passing through Native American lands and ignited new conflicts.

On October 5, 1855, following several deadly encounters, a company of 84 soldiers under the command of Major Granville O. Haller marched north from the Dalles, Oregon, to the Yakima Valley to bring order to the region. The troops encountered some 300 warriors under the direction of Yakama Chief Kamiakin near present-day Toppenish, and the two groups exchanged shots. This battle, which was followed on November 9 by the Battle of Two Buttes, south of present-day Union Gap, marked the start of what became known as the Yakama (or Yakima) War, a three-year series of skirmishes between the tribes and U.S. military forces. The war finally ended in September 1858, when tribal fighters were decisively defeated at the Battle of Four Lakes, on a tributary of the Spokane River.

It was during the war that Col. George Wright established Fort Simcoe. He assigned Maj. Robert Seldon Garnett to begin construction of the fort in the foothills of the Cascade Mountains, near the base of the Simcoe Mountains, in the summer of 1856. The fort's usefulness as a military installation, however, was short-lived. On April 17, 1859, the fort's troops received orders relocating them to other installations. The 21 buildings

The Gothic-style Commander's House at Fort Simcoe Historical State Park, constructed in 1856, is one of the oldest surviving buildings at the former military fort.

This wooden guardhouse at Fort Simcoe is one of a handful of reconstructed buildings found in the park.

of the fort were transferred to the Yakama Indian Agency, part of the Bureau of Indian Affairs, and an Indian boarding school was established on the grounds.

Girls' and boys' dormitory buildings were erected northeast of the fort's parade grounds, with a church between the two residence halls converted into classrooms, according to historical records. The first students at the school, which taught children through about seventh grade, arrived in April 1861. The students were instructed in reading, writing, and trade skills such as carpentry and blacksmithing.

In conformance with federal law at the time, the children in the school were not permitted to wear traditional clothing, speak their native languages, or follow their traditional religious practices. Students were even given English names to replace their native ones.

During this time, several of the military buildings were torn down, the parade ground was converted into a garden and orchard, tended by the students, and the former officers' quarters were used as agency offices. Additionally, a brick commissary was built near the dormitories. The school operated until 1920, closing after a fire destroyed the classrooms in December 1919. The abandoned dormitory structures were demolished in the 1950s.

In 1923 the Indian agency relocated to Toppenish, and the property sat unused for many years, although there was an effort to preserve it in the late 1930s. In 1949 another fire destroyed the last remaining original barracks and several storehouses. In 1956 the Yakama tribe granted a 99-year lease to the Washington State Parks and Recreation Commission to preserve the 196-acre site as a historic monument. In 1974 it was placed on the National Register of Historic Places.

Since then, the Washington State Parks and Recreation Commission has restored the six original buildings still standing on the site, including the Gothic-inspired Commander's House, three surrounding Captains' houses, a blockhouse, and the former jail and guardhouse. The original commissary was converted into an interpretive center (not open at this writing).

Additionally, the state parks commission has reconstructed several buildings, including the barracks, several blockhouses, a sentry house, and a guardhouse. More recently, the Yakama Nation has begun working with the park system to develop a more complete picture of the fort's history, including its dark past. It also hopes to eventually develop an institution highlighting Yakama culture, traditions, and language.

36
Manhattan Project National Historic Park

46.3851° N, 119.3555° W

On Logston Boulevard in Hanford, 21 miles north of Richland

The nondescript building in which the plutonium used in the first atomic bomb was made is a jumble of building-block-style square walls that look more industrial than elegant. But that's not at all surprising given the concrete structure was built to contain one of the most top-secret projects in American history. Located in Hanford, about 20 miles north of Richland, is the Manhattan Project National Historic Park, a collection of buildings that help tell the story of America's effort to design and manufacture a viable atomic bomb during World War II.

B Reactor, built in about 11 months between 1943 and 1944, was the first large-scale nuclear reactor ever constructed. Using technologies that were, in many cases, invented especially for the facility, its purpose was to convert natural uranium into plutonium-239, which could be used in nuclear weapons.

During the war, many scientists and politicians feared that the Germans, who counted some of the world's top physicists in their ranks, would be the first to develop a nuclear bomb with vast destructive capabilities. Even legendary physicist Albert Einstein, who was no fan of war or weapons, had written a letter in October 1939 urging President Franklin D. Roosevelt to initiate efforts to stockpile the raw materials such a bomb would require and "speed up the experimental work" on developing the technology for the bombs. He said it was imperative to do so before an atomic bomb could be developed by the Germans.

By 1942 the American government had created what became known as the Manhattan Project. Following a successful demonstration proving that a nuclear reaction could safely occur, conducted beneath a football stadium grandstand at the University of Chicago, the U.S. embarked on a three-pronged approach to develop a usable bomb.

A 600-square-mile site in Hanford, on the Columbia River, was selected for a secret factory that would make the plutonium needed for the weapon. Another secret complex in Oak Ridge, Tennessee, was constructed to enrich uranium, while a covert laboratory in Los Alamos, New Mexico, would build and test the bomb. The government chose Hanford because of its remoteness and its accessibility to the river, which provided an abundant supply of the cold water needed to cool the reactors, as well as ample hydroelectric power.

B Reactor was the first of nine reactors eventually constructed at the Hanford site, which ultimately included more than 60 buildings. B Reactor operated from September 1944 until it was permanently shut down in February 1968. The last Hanford reactor, N Reactor, was built in 1963 and operated until 1987.

Over the past several decades, most of the Hanford reactors have been "cocooned," meaning the structures were dismantled and the sites were sealed. One of the exceptions was B Reactor, which was added to the National Register of Historic Places in 1992 and designated a national historic landmark in 2008. Later, in 2011, it became part of the Manhattan Project National Historical Park.

In recent years, the National Park Service, aided by knowledgeable local volunteers, has offered public tours of B Reactor on selected dates from April to November. The four-hour tour, which is free but requires preregistration, begins with a

Exterior of B Reactor at the Manhattan Project National Historic Park. The building houses the first large-scale nuclear reactor ever constructed, and produced the plutonium that was used to create the first atom bombs during World War II.

short movie at the Manhattan Project Park visitor center, at 2000 Logston Blvd. in Richland, followed by a 25-mile bus ride to the reactor. Once at the site, visitors are given a short walking tour of the reactor building and then are permitted to wander the site to view various displays and placards describing the equipment, safety protocols, and other aspects of the reactor's history and operations.

Perhaps the most impressive part of the tour is the main reactor room, where visitors can view a massive wall containing 2,004 fuel tubes (now inert) that once contained uranium fuel. These tubes were the heart of the reactor process. Visitors can also view the control room, where the entire operation was managed, as well as the storage area, where spent uranium was discharged, and various workrooms.

The park service also offers a free public tour of the Hanford area, called the Pre-Manhattan Tour, which takes visitors to the area's pre-World War II sites. This tour focuses on the history of Native American activity in the region as well as early settler populations, including the history of the former towns of Hanford and White Bluffs, which were depopulated in 1943 so the federal government could develop the atomic program.

The Valve Pit, which housed the main connections and control valves for the water lines used to cool the reactor.

37
James Moore Mansion

46.2285° N, 119.1358° W

On North Road 34 in Pasco/Tri-Cities area

Nestled beneath the Pioneer Memorial Bridge, also called the Blue Bridge, which links Pasco to Kennewick, the elegant Moore Mansion is a testament to its builder, wealthy businessman and developer James A. Moore, who was also responsible for Seattle's prestigious Capitol Hill neighborhood.

At the start of the 20th century, Moore, who had made his fortune in Canada working with his father in ship-building and shipping before finding success as a real estate investor, turned his attention to farming and ranching in eastern Washington (later he would invest in a steel mill and in several mining operations). It was said that the reason Moore chose Pasco was that he had been told the area's drier climate would better suit his wife, Bessie, who suffered from tuberculosis.

Interested in irrigation and reclaiming desert lands, Moore decided to establish a model farm project in the Tri-Cities area. By 1905 Moore had more than 1,000 acres under irrigation in Pasco, along with five barns, an assortment of outbuildings, several massive irrigation pumps, and 200 cows. As part of his project, in 1908 Moore began construction on a showcase residence in Pasco that would reinforce the economic viability and prosperity of the area.

Eventually known as the Moore Mansion, the four-story residence (later reduced to three stories), built in the Beaux Arts architectural style, boasted a sandstone foundation, 42 rooms, two fireplaces, and large porches on both the first and second floor. The National Register nomination form for the property noted that the porches "add a touch of graciousness reminiscent of mansions in the deep south."

The house incorporated materials from a hotel, the Washington Hotel (previously known as the Hotel Denny), that Moore owned in Seattle. That Victorian-style hotel, which had a commanding view of the city, had once been considered the grandest hotel in the West, but it was dismantled during the regrading of the surrounding hill (Denny Hill).

Unfortunately, Bessie Moore died in September 1908, before she could move into the mansion. James Moore declined to live in the home following her death, and in 1911 he sold it, along with some of the surrounding land, to Thomas Carstens, who owned a successful local meat-packing business. Carstens permitted his resident manager, Otto Richter, and his family to live in the house from about 1914 to 1921.

For much of the 1920s, the mansion was owned by a local dairy farmer, who built a barn and milk house on an adjacent property. About 1930, a new owner converted the house into a speakeasy, serving moonshine and offering live entertainment. During that time, a tunnel was built from the basement of the house to the Columbia River, so guests arriving by boat could be privately guided upstairs, through a trap door and passageway, to a fourth-floor "recreation room."

According to records, the house was part of a ranching operation in the late 1930s and, during the 1940s, it served as a boardinghouse for migrant workers. In 1948 it was converted into a nursing home. By the early 1970s, however, the grand mansion had largely been abandoned, although news accounts of the time report that it was inhabited by about a dozen "hippies," who apparently hosted a memorable New

The elegant Beaux Arts-style Moore Mansion in Pasco was built in 1908 by wealthy businessman James A. Moore.

Year's Eve party that attracted more than 1,000 people before being closed down by police. Placed on the National Register of Historic Places in 1979, the home was partially restored and, from 1989 to 1995, it was used as a restaurant.

By the late 1990s, the house was again vacant, and in 2001 it was almost destroyed by a fire believed to be the work of an arsonist. Damage to the mansion included the destruction of the roof and part of the attic, which led to later rain damage to the building.

In 2004, just as city officials were preparing to issue a demolition order, it was purchased by retired Air Force Lt. Col. Brad Peck and his wife, Debra, who painstakingly rebuilt and restored the deteriorated house as a private residence and a venue for weddings, proms, and other gatherings. The Becks also added a separate events center and other structures to the six-acre property. In 2020 it was acquired by Sandrine and Thomas King, who have continued using it as their home and as a special-events facility for functions such as weddings, bridal shows, quinceañeras, and corporate parties.

38
Maryhill Museum of Art

45.6776° N, 120.8648° W

13 miles southwest of Goldendale via US 97 and WA State Route 14

Businessman Samuel (Sam) Hill (whom we met in Part I) was a "big idea" person. Hill, who had started out in a legal career and later became a successful Midwestern railroad executive and financier, first visited the Pacific Northwest in early 1890s when his railroad, the Great Northern Railway, was expanding into Seattle. He quickly saw promise in the booming port town and began investing in a local gas and electric company.

In 1895 Hill decided to leave the railroad company to pursue other financial opportunities. By the early 1900s, with the advent of the internal-combustion engine, he had become convinced that quality roads were essential for the country to thrive. Along with like-minded businessmen and politicians, he helped form the Washington State Good Roads Association to promote the development and construction of better roadways.

Around the same time, Hill, who had been born into a Quaker family, purchased a large swath of land near the eastern edge of the Columbia Gorge to develop into a utopian agricultural oasis. As a railroad insider, he had learned the Spokane, Portland and Seattle Railroad planned to lay tracks along the Washington side of the gorge, so the region would have access to rail service. He also believed that the site, sitting between the rainy climate of western Washington and drier eastern Washington, would be perfect for growing crops and supporting his concept of an agricultural paradise. His plan was to sell substantial plots of the land—he would eventually purchase some 7,000 acres—to Quaker farmers.

On this property Hill laid out a 34-block townsite, which he named Maryhill, after his wife and daughter (who shared the name Mary), and built a church, a hotel, a store, offices, garages, and shops, along with 10 miles of paved roads. He also, in 1914, began work on a massive Beaux-Arts-style mansion on a plateau about 3 miles from the town of Maryhill. This grand structure, designed by the prestigious Washington, D.C.-based firm Hornblower and Marshall, would be not only his family home but also a stylish place to entertain his friends and acquaintances, which included several members of European royalty.

Unfortunately for Hill, while the land directly adjacent to the Columbia River was fertile and productive, all of the land above that narrow growing zone was too rocky and wind-swept to be agriculturally productive. Not surprisingly, Maryhill land sales never took off, and Hill was forced to revise his plans. He tried to raise cattle on the property, and he operated a ferry service for a short time (neither were profitable).

The outbreak of World War I placed new limitations on Hill's financial opportunities. By 1917 he had abandoned his plans for developing Maryhill and slowed work on the mansion. Hill's money woes were resolved later that year when he sold a small Portland telephone and telegraph company that he owned to the much larger Bell Systems Portland Telephone & Telegraph Company.

With his new wealth, Hill began an unprecedented building spree. During the war, he had begun to envision constructing a full-size replica of Stonehenge as a tribute to the soldiers and sailors of Klickitat County who had given their lives to the war effort. The massive circle of stones, designed to look like the 4,000-year-old English landmark, was not completed until 1930. Still standing, the unusual memorial is located about two miles east of the Maryhill Mansion. He also decided to erect a peace monument to commemorate a century of good relations between the U.S. and its northern neighbor, Canada, which was built on the border between the two countries (featured in Part I). The imposing Peace Arch was completed in 1921.

Constructed between 1914 and 1940, the Maryhill Museum was the brainchild of businessman Samuel Hill, who initially intended it to serve as a showcase home overlooking the Columbia River before repurposing it as a museum. Today, it houses an impressive collection of international artwork and antiquities.

As for his Maryhill mansion, Hill was persuaded by a good friend, modern-dance pioneer Loie Fuller, to complete the 60-by-93-foot structure and convert it into a world-class art museum. Despite the house being only half-completed, in 1926 Hill hosted a museum dedication—which included a speech by his friend, Queen Marie of Romania—that attracted more than 2,000 people. The museum would not be open to the public, however, for another 14 years.

Throughout the rest of his life, Hill proved reluctant to complete construction of the museum because he was frustrated that the state of Washington had not completed the promised construction of the highway on the north bank of the Columbia River. The highway would be completed in 1931, shortly after Hill died (his ashes are buried in a crypt just below the Stonehenge Memorial). Over the next decade, the museum's trustees, under the guidance of Hill's good friend, Alma de Bretteville Spreckels, wife of San Francisco sugar magnate Adolph Spreckels, marshalled the resources to complete the building.

The Maryhill Museum of Art finally opened to the public on May 13, 1940. Its eclectic collection still includes more than 80 original bronze and plaster casts by Auguste Rodin, as well as Tanagra figures donated by the Queen of Greece; antiquities from Crete; European and American paintings of the 19th and 20th centuries; the Royal Romanian throne from the Summer Palace; and Native American art.

The museum was added to the National Register of Historic Places in 1974. In 2012 the museum was expanded when the Mary and Bruce Stevenson Wing was added to the building's southern side.

39
Wishram Indian Village Site

45.6427° N, 121.1056° W

6 miles east of Dallesport on WA State Route 14

The village of the Wishram people was the largest settlement at the eastern edge of the Columbia Gorge, according to the famed explorers Meriwether Lewis and William Clark. Residents resided in several dozen mat lodges (housing made of woven-grass mats) as well as in wooden structures that were partly underground. The village was located on the Columbia River's north bank, roughly across from what today we call The Dalles.

Known in the Wishram language as *Nixluidix* or "the trading place," the settlement was a seasonal camping site where members of several Pacific Northwest tribes, including the Wishram, gathered to fish salmon, trade goods, share news, and mingle. Clark, in fact, called it the "Great Mart."

Lewis and Clark briefly stayed at Nixluidix in October 1805, on their westward journey to the Pacific, and in April 1806, during their return trip east. The explorers, who noted that they were warmly received by the Wishram, were able to trade with the tribe for fresh horses. During their April visit, they also witnessed the sacred First Fish Ceremony, which celebrated the annual coming of the salmon in spring. Lewis described how the Wishram people exhibited "great joy" with the arrival of the fish, which was one of their most important food sources.

The Wishram were at the center of an extensive indigenous peoples' trade network. The tribe served as an important link between the tribes living along the Pacific Coast and the inland tribes from as far away as Idaho and beyond. As a trading society, the Wishram spoke several languages, including their own tongue (Wasco-Wishram, a form of Chinookan), the Sahaptian language of the tribes to the east, and a Chinookan trade language known as Chinook Wawa.

Archeological evidence indicates that the settlement, which Clark estimated had a population of more than 1,000 during his April 1806 visit, was 10,000 to 15,000 years old. As with many native communities, the increasing number of non-indigenous people traveling through the area during the next several decades ultimately led to its downfall. In 1841 the village had a population of about 400 people living in some 40 wooden lodges, and that number was greatly reduced following a smallpox outbreak in 1854.

In 1860, under the terms of the Yakama treaty of 1855, the remaining members of the Wishram tribe were forced to relocate to the Yakama Indian Reservation or the Warm Springs Indian Reservation in Oregon. The treaty did permit them to continue fishing on the Columbia River, but they could no longer reside on their ancestral lands.

In the late 19th and early 20th centuries, the area around the Wishram village site was divided into several large, white-owned ranches, and a two-lane highway, now known as Washington State Route 14, was constructed over the site. In the 1950s, the federal government funded construction of The Dalles Dam, a massive concrete structure that would supply hydroelectric power for the Pacific Northwest. After the dam was completed in 1957, the water behind the dam submerged the Wishram village site, which had become known as Spearfish. as well as Celilo Falls, once an important tribal fishing area on the Columbia River.

The rising water behind the dam, which formed a large reservoir known as Horsethief Lake, also swallowed an adjacent canyon that contained panels of ancient rock art, called petroglyphs, which had been carved into the stone walls thousands of years ago. In response, the tribes worked with federal officials to save about 40 of the rock art panels, which were jackhammered out of the canyon cliffs. After languishing for many years in storage, the stone artwork was placed in a permanent outdoor display called *Tamani Pesh-Wa,* or "Written on the Rock," when the Columbia Hills Historical State Park was established in 2003 (the park encompasses the former Horsethief Lake State Park and Dalles Mountain Ranch).

View of Horsethief Butte from the Columbia River. This area was once the site of a thriving village of the Wishram people. The site was submerged when The Dalles Dam was constructed in the 1950s. It is now part of Columbia Hills Historic State Park.

Inset: *Petroglyphs, or prehistoric Native American rock art, could once be found in a canyon near the Wishram village. A number of rock art panels, like this one, were removed from the canyon and are on display in the park.*

Among the preserved petroglyphs is a carved image known as *Tsagiglalal* or "She Who Watches." The striking image with two large, almost hypnotic eyes is said to be of a female chief of the tribe who was turned into stone by Coyote the trickster god because she defied him. Considered a sacred figure, Tsagiglala, as well as a handful of other petroglyphs and pictographs, can only be viewed by guided tour, which is offered on Saturdays between April and October.

The park, which spans 3,338 acres, also includes Horsethief Lake and Horsethief Butte, an imposing rock formation that overlooks the lake and was also an important gathering place for the Wishram and other tribes. Marked trails lead visitors to the top of the butte, which offers spectacular views of the gorge. Interestingly, the name "Horsethief" was not bestowed on these various local places because of any illegal activities, but because, in the 1950s, U.S. Army Corps of Engineers workers developing the dam site thought the area resembled the type of terrain where horse thieves often hid out in old western films.

Despite being submerged, the Wishram Indian Village was added to the National Historic Register in 1972 s an important historical cultural site.

Spokane's Great Northern Clocktower, which overlooks the Spokane River, was once attached to the Great Northern Railway Depot (demolished in the early 1970s). Both were built in 1902 and are reminders of the important role railroads played in the development of Spokane.

EAST

Much like the central part of the state, eastern Washington owes a lot to irrigation and agriculture. Because of its fertile and seemingly endless rolling hills, largely planted with wheat and wine grapes, it has been called Washington's bread basket. Interestingly, those hills, called the Palouse, are the result of tens of thousands of years of dust and silt, known as "loess," being blown into mounds.

The largest city in eastern Washington is Spokane, with a population of more than 230,000, which makes it the state's second-largest city. The region was home of the indigenous Spokan or Spokane people (the name is commonly believed to mean "Children of the Sun"), who were sustained by the salmon-filled rivers and plentiful game in the area.

The first non-indigenous people to arrive were fur traders and missionaries, who came in the early part of the 19th century. In 1871 James J. Downing and Seth R. Scranton built a sawmill on the Spokane River adjacent to beautiful Spokane Falls. Two years later, James N. Glover and Jasper N. Matheney came to the area seeking land. They purchased the Downing Mill and, later, Glover acquired Scranton's holdings.

Glover, who became known as the "Father of Spokane," bought Matheney out in 1877 and brought in Frederick Post to build a gristmill at the falls. From there, he expanded his sawmill, built a general store, and began encouraging settlement on the south side of the river. Within a few years, the city of Spokane was established.

Part of the reason for Spokane's success as a commercial hub was its location near the productive wheatfields of the Palouse hills to the south as well as its access to the river. Additionally, the region's plentiful forests proved to be a boon for the development of railroads that were built through the area. In 1883 the transcontinental Northern Pacific Railway reached Spokane, connecting it to the rest of the country.

Eastern Washington also boasts a number of colleges and universities. Washington's second largest university—and the largest in eastern Washington—is Washington State University, which was founded in 1890 as the Agricultural College, Experiment Station and School of Science of the State of Washington. Located in Pullman, which is about 75 miles south of Spokane, WSU was one of the first land-grant colleges in the American West. Eastern Washington is also home to Gonzaga University and Whitworth University (in Spokane), Eastern Washington University (in Cheney), and Whitman College and Walla Walla University (in Walla Walla area).

40
Ritzville Carnegie Library

47.1263° N, 118.3821° W

On Main Avenue in Ritzville

If not for a pair of Scotsmen, the remote agricultural settlement of Ritzville might never have had its own library. One of those men was a prominent local farmer, who decided to donate his personal collection of books to the community to help start a library. The other was a fabulously wealthy industrialist, who donated much of his fortune financing the construction of libraries throughout the U.S. between 1883 and 1929.

The farmer was Daniel Buchanan, who was one of the first non-native settlers in Adams County. Buchanan was born in Glasgow, Scotland, in 1820 and, after traveling to the U.S. in 1850, arrived in Adams County in 1884. After purchasing some 800 acres land, Buchanan became a successful wheat farmer and was involved in local and state politics for many years. According to the *Adams County News*, Buchanan sold his land in October 1901, "on account of his advanced age—82 years—and no doubt he feels entitled to rest after such a long, active and well spent life."

A year later, Buchanan decided to donate his personal library of 368 books to the community of Ritzville to help start a free library and reading room. The nascent institution was initially located in a room above a local store.

The industrialist was Andrew Carnegie, who was born in Dunfermline, Scotland, in 1835. After emigrating to the U.S. at the age of 12, he made a series of shrewd investments, particularly in the booming steel industry, that resulted in him becoming one of the richest men in the world at the time. After selling off his Carnegie Steel Company for more than $300 million (the equivalent of $11 billion in today's dollars), he devoted the rest of his life to philanthropy, including building more than 2,500 libraries in the U.S., Great Britain, Canada, Ireland, Scotland, and a half dozen other countries.

Fortunately for the people of Ritzville, one of those Carnegie libraries (a total of 43 were built in the state of Washington, with 32 still standing) would be located in their community. In 1904 Ritzville sought a Carnegie Foundation grant to finance the construction of a library building and, in anticipation of receiving the money, approved a ballot proposition to pay for land acquisition and to fund ongoing operations.

Two years later, the foundation agreed to grant the community $10,500 to build a library, provided the community contribute $1,000 annually for its operations and books. At the time, Ritzville was the smallest town in the entire country to receive funding from the Carnegie Foundation for such a project.

The buff-colored brick library was constructed in 1907. The completed one-story, rectangular structure, which boasted high ceilings and a large basement, was designed by a well-known Spokane architectural firm, Preusse and Zittel. A noteworthy element in the building's design is the band of fine corbelling (the decorative use of overlapping bricks) around the structure just below the roofline. Initially, the building served not only as the town library but also a place for community meetings (in its basement), including the Ritzville City Council and a number of civic organizations.

The library, built in what has been described as a restrained Neoclassical style, has remained largely unchanged since it was constructed. It was listed on the National Register of Historic Places in 1980. According to a December 2022 article in the *Columbia Basin News*, the library still stacks books on wooden shelves installed in 1907 and has its original wooden floors and stairs. One of the few modern additions: an elevator between the basement and first floor was added in 2017.

Built in 1907, the Ritzville Library, funded by the Carnegie Foundation, long served as an important community meeting place.

41
Monroe Street Bridge

47.6606° N, 117.4267° W

On Monroe Street in downtown Spokane

One of Spokane's most iconic structures is the magnificent Monroe Street Bridge, which spans the Spokane River in the city's downtown. When it was built, from 1910 to 1911, it was the largest arched concrete bridge in the U.S. and the third-largest in the world. The massive, 896-foot-long structure, which stands 135 feet above beautiful Spokane Falls, was constructed using 7,100 cubic yards of concrete and 500 tons of reinforcing steel. The original cost of the bridge was $535,000 (about $17.7 million in today's dollars), and more than 240,000 man-hours of work went into its construction.

The current bridge is actually the third to be built on that site. The original Monroe Street span was a wood structure constructed in 1889 by the Spokane Cable Railway, primarily for its electric streetcars. It burned about a year after being completed, reportedly due to overheated electric cables interlaced in the bridge's wooden frame.

A second bridge, made of steel, soon replaced it in 1892, but traveling across that structure on a streetcar was considered a particularly frightening experience because the bridge was so poorly constructed that it shook and vibrated tremendously. The *Spokesman Review* newspaper noted that in 1907, when the Ringling Brothers Circus was in town, it tried to hold a parade through the city with all its elephants. However, when the animals reached the bridge, they reportedly refused to cross it.

That same year, 1907, William H. Burr, a noted engineer with the National Good Roads Association, wrote an analysis of the bridge that indicated it simply wasn't safe. He said the steel used in its construction wasn't strong enough for such a long expanse and the foundations were not adequate. Following Burr's report, the city closed the bridge in July 1910 and agreed to replace it with something more substantial that would better serve the community.

With that, the third—and current—Monroe Street Bridge, which was designed by Spokane City Engineer John Chester Ralston, began to take shape. The reinforced concrete bridge, which took less than a year and a half to complete, incorporated design flourishes such as decorative concrete bison heads, covered pavilions, and a chain-link railing motif. According to historical records, the bridge's decked arch design was inspired by the new Rocky River Bridge in Ohio, built between 1908 and 1910. (That bridge stood until 1971, when it was replaced by a larger one.)

In 1914 Spokane officials gave their approval for the Great Northern Railway to construct a giant railroad bridge on top of the concrete bridge's north side. The result, according to historians, was a huge, looming steel structure that many thought took away from the Monroe Street Bridge's attractiveness. The visually overbearing railroad bridge was finally removed in 1974 as part of the city's preparations for Spokane's Expo 74. Other changes were made over the years as well. In 1925 the bridge's gas lamps were converted to electricity, and in 1934 the electric streetcar line was removed.

In recognition of its historical importance to the city of Spokane, the Monroe Street Bridge was listed on the National Register of Historic Places in 1976. In the 1990s, however, after chunks of concrete fell from the bridge into the river, it became increasingly apparent that the 80-year-old structure

When it was completed in 1911, Spokane's Monroe Street Bridge was the largest arched concrete bridge in America and the third largest in the world.

was badly in need of repairs. From January 2003 to September 2005, the bridge was closed for an $18 million reconstruction project, which included replacing decaying and outmoded materials and rebuilding it to its original appearance.

When the bridge reopened, the *Spokesman-Review* proclaimed,

> The mammoth, 94-year-old concrete Monroe Street Bridge has borne witness to Spokane history from the Roaring '20s, through the Great Depression, World War II, Expo '74 and beyond. But by the turn of the 21st century, years of spraying water and pounding traffic had battered the bridge to just a shadow of its former glory.
>
> This weekend Spokane will celebrate the bridge's rebirth as it reopens after a 2 1/3-year restoration project that stripped the structure down to its bare bones and rebuilt it sturdy enough to last another 75 years.

42
Patsy Clark Mansion

47.3919° N, 117.2639° W

2208 West Second Avenue, in Spokane's Browne's Addition neighborhood

Even in the prestigious and historic Browne's Addition neighborhood, west of Spokane's city center, the Patsy Clark Mansion is a rare gem. It was added to the National Register of Historic Places in 1975, while the neighborhood itself, which is the oldest in the city, was listed a year later.

A large part of what makes the Clark Mansion noteworthy is its one-of-a-kind architectural design. The structure was described on its nomination form as "an eclectic blur of styles bearing little resemblance to any of the more standard architectural types found elsewhere in Browne's Addition." The nomination added that while specific influences might be recognizable in some of the home's details, as a whole the building is "apparently an original conception of the architect's flamboyant imagination."

The two-and-a-half-story brick building, located opposite shady Coeur d'Alene Park, was built in 1898 for Patrick "Patsy" Clark, an Irish immigrant who made a vast fortune in mining, primarily in Montana, Utah, Idaho, Canada, and Mexico. Clark arrived in Spokane in 1887 to oversee his mining interests in the nearby Coeur d'Alene district in Idaho. In 1889, after the home he was living in burned during the Great Fire of Spokane, Clark decided to build an even grander residence.

Clark hired Kirtland K. Cutter, one of the city's best known and most visionary architects to design his new mansion. He told the architect that he wanted "to create the most impressive house west of the Mississippi" and is said to have put no restrictions on cost. In response, Cutter traveled throughout the U.S. and Europe to get ideas, select building materials, and hire talented craftsmen to work on the project.

At the time, Spokane was recovering from the Great Fire, which had destroyed a significant part of the city. This presented Cutter, and other architects and builders working to rebuild the city, with a blank canvas on which to create a new Spokane. The late 19th century was a time when Spokane experienced its own version of the Gilded Age. Businessmen who made fortunes in railroading, mining, agriculture, and lumber wanted to build mansions that exemplified their financial successes. Many of these homes were built in Spokane's Browne's Addition neighborhood.

Work was completed on Clark's 11,422-square-foot mansion, which has a vaguely Moorish appearance, in 1898. Cutter's designs called for each major room to be built in an entirely different architectural style, with each constructed using the most expensive materials and craftsmanship. For example, the French drawing room features ceiling frescoes, a wide base-relief frieze, Corinthian columns, silk wall covers, and a marble fireplace. The foyer boasts a nine-foot-tall grandfather clock, fumed oak woodwork, and gold-embossed red Spanish leather wall coverings.

The dining room, meanwhile, has a Medieval English motif with high wainscoting, exposed ceiling beams, and 27 hand-carved monks' heads, each with a different expression. The 16-piece dining room furniture set was designed by Cutter and made in Connecticut. At the top of the stairs leading to the second floor is a 14-foot-tall, 8-foot-wide leaded-glass window with a delicate peacock design in amber and indigo, made by the Tiffany Studios in New York.

The second floor of the house originally served as bedrooms, each with a fireplace, while the third floor contained the maid's quarters and a ballroom. At the rear of the house is a two-story brick carriage house.

Clark resided in the mansion until his death of a heart attack in 1915, at the age of 64. His wife, Ann, continued living in the house until her death in 1926. The mansion was then sold that year to Eugene Enloe, who lived in it with his family until 1946. During the next several decades, the mansion was used as a hotel then, after being renovated, served as a restaurant from 1982 to 2001. In recent years, it has been largely restored to its original appearance and houses a prominent local law firm.

With its eclectic blend of architectural styles, the Patsy Clark mansion is one of the more impressive homes found in Spokane's historic Browne's Addition neighborhood.

43
Benewah Milk Bottle

47.652778° N, 117.432222° W

On Cedar Street in downtown Spokane

There is not much distinctive about the rectangular row of buildings across the street from the majestic First Presbyterian Church in downtown Spokane—except for one that is shaped like a giant white milk bottle. Known as the Benewah Milk Bottle (after the creamery company that built it), the 38-foot-tall and 15-foot-wide, bottle-shaped structure was constructed in 1935 by local contractor W. G. Myers for Paul E. Newport, who owned the dairy company.

Newport wanted a distinctive retail outlet from which to sell his Benewah Creamery-branded dairy products. A year earlier, he had already built his first bottle-shaped structure, on the corner of Garland and Post streets in north Spokane. That building, known as the Garland Milk Bottle, was severely damaged by fire in 2011 but has been completely rebuilt. It currently serves as a popular ice cream parlor. Unlike its twin, the Garland Milk Bottle is not listed on the National Register of Historic Places.

Newport had named his company after the county of his birth, Benewah County, Idaho (which, in turn, was named to honor Coeur d'Alene tribal chief Benewah). A few years after starting his dairy business in Idaho, Newport moved to Spokane in 1922. His first production facility here, which included a store, was located at First and Washington streets. Eventually, he had retail outlets throughout the city, including the two milk-bottle buildings. Newport originally planned to build six such structures, but it is believed he abandoned the idea with the advent of the Great Depression.

The Benewah Milk Bottle on Cedar Street was the work of the well-known Spokane architectural firm Whitehouse and Price. That firm was also responsible for the Hutton Settlement orphanage complex in Spokane and several buildings on the University of Washington campus in Seattle.

The building's architectural style has been described as "mimetic," meaning it is a literal design that combines form with function, allowing the building itself to serve as its own best promotional vehicle. It was constructed using a contoured wood frame covered with stucco. At the neck and cap, the wood frame was covered with sheet metal. The building also had three windows placed symmetrically on either side of a wooden front door. For most of its existence, the bottle was painted white with a blue cap and had neon lighting to highlight the contours of the structure.

Originally, the two Milk Bottles, which each cost about $3,700 (or nearly $87,000 in today's dollars), served as factory outlets for Benewah Creamery products. Newport sold his own dairy products directly to the public at a lower price than his retail competitors. To chill the products, a refrigeration unit and storage area were attached to the rear of the giant bottle structures.

The two bottle buildings remained in use as retail outlets for the creamery until 1974, when the company was sold to a larger dairy conglomerate. In later years, the Cedar Street Benewah building was used for storage, as an office, as the headquarters for the local Democratic Party, as a physical-therapy clinic, and, more recently, as the box office for a local improv theater company. It was added to the National Register of Historic Places in 1986.

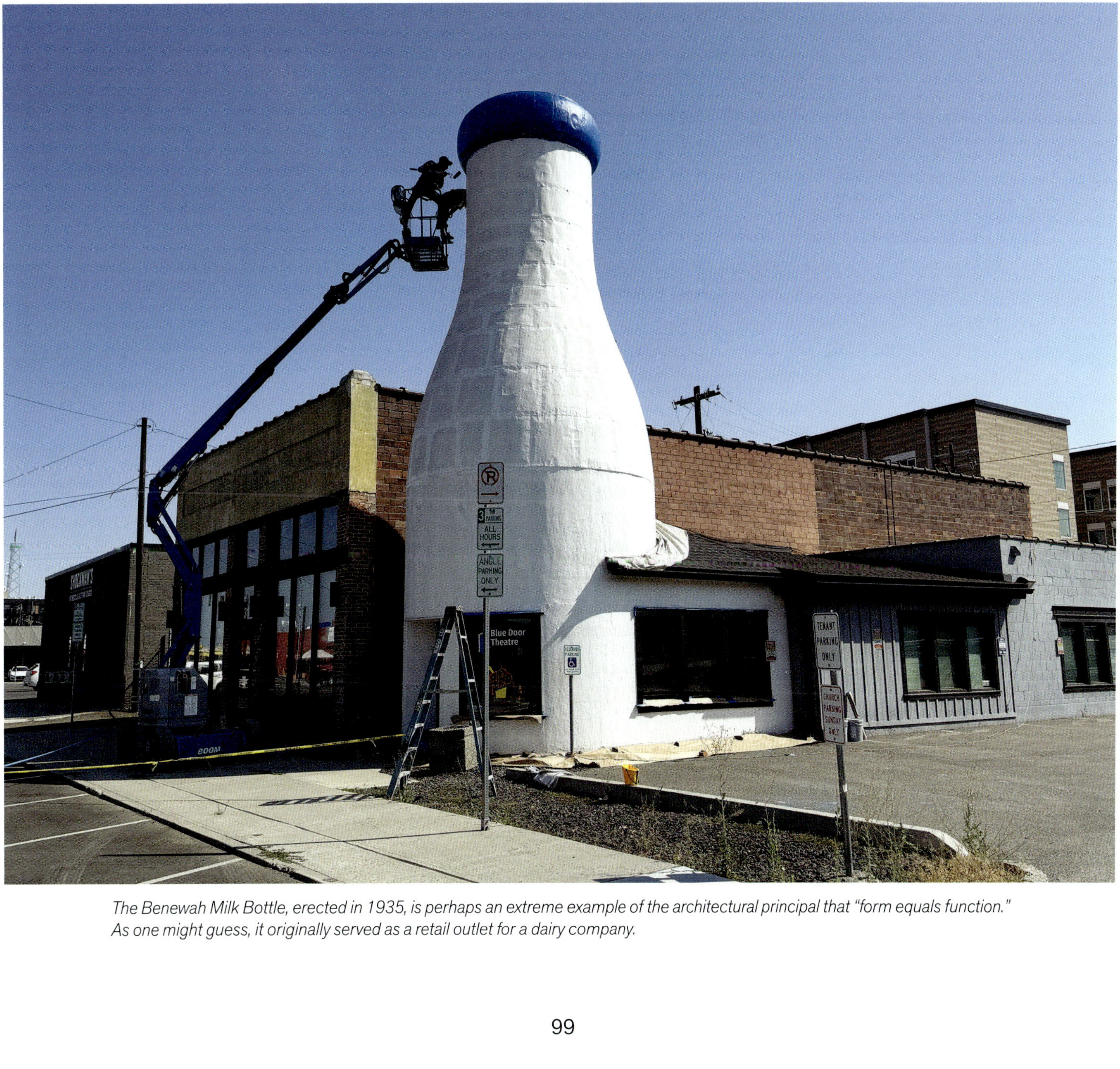

The Benewah Milk Bottle, erected in 1935, is perhaps an extreme example of the architectural principal that "form equals function." As one might guess, it originally served as a retail outlet for a dairy company.

44

Steptoe Battlefield State Park Heritage Site

47.2286° N, 117.3650° W

On South Summit Loop in Rosalia

In the late 1850s, tensions were high between the native tribes in what would become the state of Washington and the growing number of white settlers and miners entering the territory. In the eastern part of the state, members of the Spokan, Palus, and Coeur d' Alene tribes grew increasingly concerned about the newcomers, who were pushing them out of their traditional hunting, fishing, and camping grounds.

The discovery of gold in British Columbia in the mid-1850s brought in a wave of miners, who ignored any treaties or agreements the government had made with native tribes. One of those treaties, the Walla Walla Treaty of 1855, had forbidden whites from trespassing onto native lands unless invited by the tribes. Unfortunately, the treaty was tied up in Congress for several years, so many did not believe it was in effect.

In response to the situation, the U.S. government stationed troops throughout the Washington Territory to protect settlers and miners. Often this meant pacifying and, typically, removing the natives. One such military company was the 9th Infantry Regiment led by Lt. Col. Edward J. Steptoe, a West Point graduate and veteran of the Seminole War and the Mexican-American War. Steptoe had become the commander of Fort Walla Walla in 1854, tasked with keeping the peace between the native people and the new arrivals.

On May 6, 1858, Steptoe led about 160 lightly-armed men, along with some 30 packers and a handful of Nez Perce scouts, accompanied by a train of horses, cattle, and mules packed with supplies and equipment, to Fort Colville. Tensions were high in the area, where the military was planning to build a road, and Steptoe hoped a show of force would intimidate the natives.

After traveling for about a week, the company reached Pine Creek, where, on May 15, they made camp. The next morning, the troops began heading north along the creek. Soon a group of armed native warriors from several tribes gathered around them to angrily insist they should not be on their land.

Steptoe, however, ignored them and continued leading his men along the creek until they reached a too-narrow spot. Realizing they could not continue that way, Steptoe ordered his troops to retreat to a small lake and attempt to move forward the next day.

On the morning of May 16, Steptoe and his troops started back the way they had come and came under fire from a force of native warriors, which had grown tremendously since the day before, to an estimated 1,000. Steptoe's company made a successful break to higher ground while the fighting grew more intense, especially when one column was nearly cut off from the main body of soldiers. Realizing he had encountered far more resistance than he anticipated, on May 17 Steptoe ordered a retreat to a nearby hill. Once there, Steptoe's troops took defensive positions and continued the fight for hours despite being surrounded on all sides and with ammunition running low.

What happened next has long been the subject of conjecture. Late that night, after the fighting was suspended, Steptoe ordered his men to bury their howitzers to prevent them from falling into the hands of the enemy, and to quietly retreat to the

This quiet hill in Rosalia is the site of the Battle of Tohotonimme, where Lt. Col. Edward J. Steptoe and his company of 160 lightly armed soldiers, along with 30 packers and a handful of scouts, retreated after facing unexpected resistance from a much larger force of Native American warriors. A tall stone monument to the battle stands in the background.

other side of the nearby Snake River. Some historians believe one of the native chiefs, who was a Christian, instructed his warriors to look the other way, while others insist Steptoe was merely fortunate that he and his troops were able to slink away virtually unnoticed. Steptoe and his surviving troops—he had lost a total of seven men, including the two officers—made their way back to Fort Walla Walla, where Steptoe quickly informed his superiors of the disastrous foray into native territory. In the short term, the battle was considered a victory for the eastern Washington tribes.

In response, however, the U.S. government ordered more than 700 heavily armed soldiers, under the leadership of Col. George Wright, to move into the area to begin the process of "Indian removal." Over that summer, this larger force defeated the tribes and ended for good their armed resistance in the region.

Today, the hill where Steptoe and his troops made their stand is the site of a large stone monument commemorating the battle, which native people call the Battle of Tohotonimme. Erected in 1914 by the Esther Reed Chapter of the Daughters of the American Revolution, it is the centerpiece of the four-acre Steptoe Battlefield State Park Heritage Site, which was established by the state in 1950. The site was added to the National Register of Historic Places in 1976.

45
J. C. Barron Flour Mill

47.1282° N, 117.2427° W

On 1st Street in Oakesdale

Few places are as representative of eastern Washington's agricultural history and heritage as the J. C. Barron Flour Mill in the small town of Oakesdale. Built in 1890, the Barron Mill was once one of 19 flour mills in eastern Washington's Whitman County. The three-and-a-half-story mill was built adjacent to the tracks of two now-defunct railroads, the Northern Pacific Railway to the west and the Spokane and Inland Railroad, which operated spur lines to the north and east. When trains stopped in front of the mill, large metal spouts that projected from the building dumped grain into awaiting cars.

In addition to the mill itself, made of rough-sawed timber with a brick foundation, the facility included a grain and flour warehouse and steam-generating plant, both completed in 1890, and a crib elevator, finished in 1898. The main mill building, which measures 40-by-68 feet, originally contained the flour- and grain-sacking machines, a small stone buhr mill, and four double stands of roller mills on the first floor. The second floor housed a tool shop and the sifting machinery while the third floor contained the flour-bleaching devices and other equipment.

According to a later owner, Mary Jane Butters, the mill, originally owned by J. G. Porter, was constructed in the eastern U.S. in 1862, but years later it was dismantled and shipped (along with the milling equipment) by rail to the young community of Oakesdale. Oakesdale was established in the mid-1880s by a man named James McCoy. For many years, it was little more than a small farming enclave. The arrival of the railroads and the mill, however, brought new prosperity to the community.

A short time after reestablishing the mill, Porter sold the buildings to Harvey Gray, who owned another mill in the nearby town of Palouse. In 1907 the mill's longtime namesake, Joseph C. Barron Sr., purchased it. Ownership would remain with his family until 1997.

Barron, a second-generation miller who was born in Pennsylvania in 1866, successfully operated the mill for more than three decades. In 1939, the mill closed because it was unable to compete with larger, interstate milling operations. However, the facility continued to be used to clean and store grain throughout World War II.

Following Barron's death in 1955, ownership of the mill transferred to his son, Joseph C. Barron Jr. The younger Barron, who was born in 1909, closed down all the aging mill's operations in 1960 for financial reasons, though he retained ownership. In 1977 the mill was added to the National Register of Historic Places.

According to a 1998 article in the Spokane *Spokesman-Review,* the younger Barron, however, couldn't get the flour business out of his system and soon began operating a smaller milling business, which catered to natural-food producers, in his garage. It was through this business that Barron came into contact with Mary Jane Butters and her husband, Nick Ogle, who operated an organic farm products company in Moscow, Idaho. In 1997 Barron, in ill health (he died in 2000), sold his company, as well as the old mill building to Butters.

Butters moved Barron's garage operation to her farm in Idaho. At the time, she told the media that she would attempt to preserve the old mill. In 2023 Butters, who had maintained the historic building for more than two decades, announced that it was for sale. In May 2024, the mill was sold to the Innovia Foundation of Spokane, a nonprofit group that works with communities to improve their quality of life, nurture the arts, and support education. The foundation said it planned to partner with the Port of Whitman County to restore the mill and develop it as community center with retail and commercial spaces. As of this writing, those efforts are ongoing.

The J. C. Barron Flour Mill in Oakesdale, built in 1890, is one of only a handful of mills still standing in eastern Washington.

46
United Presbyterian Church/ Greystone Church

46.4354° N, 117.1032° W

On Maple Street in Pullman

Not too many apartment complexes in eastern Washington can boast of once being called the finest example of Ecclesiastical architecture in the Palouse region. But that is the case with the Greystone Church Apartments in Pullman, which are housed in what was originally the United Presbyterian Church. The magnificent stone-veneer structure can trace its beginnings to the 1890s, when Washington State University (then called the Washington Agricultural College Experimental Station and School of Science) was established in Pullman.

In 1893 Enoch A. Bryan was appointed president of the new college. A devote Presbyterian, Bryan immediately recognized that the community, including the students, had a sizeable number of members of his faith, but no congregation or church. Bryan joined a group of other Presbyterians to try to establish a formal congregation in the community and raise funds for a proper house of worship.

By 1898 a plot had been purchased, and construction began on the church, which was designed by local architect William Swain, a transplant from England, who was active in Pullman civic affairs. In addition to designing many commercial buildings in Pullman, Swain was elected city clerk for several years and later served as city treasurer and as Justice of the Peace.

Swain's original wood-frame Presbyterian Church was modest in size but it easily accommodated the new parish, which counted about 40 members. Within a decade, however, the congregation had grown to the point that the church had become too small. Bryan joined with others in the congregation to raise funds to build a much larger facility. Ground was broken on the new house of worship in May 1913.

This new church was also designed by Swain. It incorporated the original, which was moved to the rear of the lot and turned 90 degrees, then faced in the same stone as the rest of the church. The enlarged United Presbyterian Church, later also known as the Greystone Church, which cost about $50,000, was built using ashlar Tenino sandstone on a base of rough-cut basalt. Constructed in the Romanesque Revival style, it was described at the time of its completion in 1914 as one of the finest examples of that style of architecture in the state.

Situated on a hillside in a residential neighborhood at the intersection of Maple Street and Maiden Lane, the church has a rectangular shape with a pair of 62-foot-tall, castle-like, crenulated towers flanking the gabled main entrance, which is to the south. Beautiful stained-glass windows line the side of the church that faces the street.

The church served Pullman's Presbyterians until 1977, when the congregation decided to build a new church in another part of town and sold the Greystone structure to the local Catholic diocese. The old stone building served as a Catholic student chapel until 1980, but then it stood vacant and unused for nearly a quarter century. In 1989 local preservationists, fearful that the empty church would be destroyed—it actually was scheduled for demolition in 2002—succeeded in getting it listed on the National Register of Historic Places.

In 2004 the church was sold to a private company, G & M Properties, which renovated and repurposed the then-90-year-old building into an apartment complex. The building was later purchased by Horizon Realty Advisers. Today, it primarily serves as housing for students at the nearby university.

This marvelous stone-veneer structure in Pullman was built in 1914 to serve as the home of the United Presbyterian Church congregation. After closing in the late 1970s and sitting vacant for many years, it was renovated into apartments in 2004.

47
Albert W. Thompson Hall

46.4353° N, 117.0957° W

On the Washington State University Campus in Pullman

One could say the elegant, red-brick-and-granite Albert W. Thompson Hall on the Washington State University campus in Pullman was locally sourced. That's because all of the bricks used to build the four-story building, with its distinctive pair of turrets, were manufactured locally using clay from a deposit found on campus, and the granite used for the basement story came from a quarry near Spokane. The presence of the clay, in fact, permitted the university to build most of its early buildings using the same type of relatively inexpensive bricks, which gave the campus a uniform appearance.

Thompson Hall, which was originally simply named "the Administration Building," is the oldest building still standing on the Pullman campus, completed in 1895. That was only three years after the college opened under its original name, the Washington State Agricultural College and School of Science (it would become the State College of Washington in 1905 and Washington State University in 1959).

Constructed using a modified Romanesque design, the building was described at its dedication as "an excellent piece of work, and one that in point of convenience, strength, and architectural beauty will compare with any state building." However, according to the Society of Architectural Historians' online encyclopedia, architecturally Thompson Hall is a bit of "an oddity" because its Romanesque look, which closely resembles a French Chateau, is unlike any of the classical or colonial revival buildings built in later years. The website dryly noted that the building's design was perhaps an attempt "to provide a dose of European civilization to a remote town on the American frontier."

Another unusual aspect of the building's design is the fact that its two front-facing turrets are not the same. One has a conical roof, while the other has a flat roof. According to campus lore, one popular explanation for the difference was that the school ran out of money to finish the flat roof with a cylindrical turret. The truth, however, is that the flat-topped tower was purposely designed that way so that meteorological instruments could be placed on a platform on the roof to help better track the weather.

Thompson Hall was designed by Seattle architects James Stephen and Timotheus Josenhans, who won a competition conducted by the university's Board of Regents. Originally the building, which cost $50,000, housed the school's administrative and faculty offices as well as laboratories and classrooms.

Over the next seven decades, the building was one of the most important on the campus. At various times, it housed the library, physical-education programs (including showers), and other departments. In 1968 the interior of the building was extensively renovated and the college administration offices were relocated to the newly constructed C. Clement French Administration Building. For several years after, the hall was technically named the Foreign Languages Building, although many simply called it the Old Administration Building.

In 1972, the year it was placed on the National Register of Historic Places, the building was officially named Albert W. Thompson Hall in honor of a longtime instructor and Dean of the College of Sciences and Art. Thompson, who was born in 1898 and died in 1994, was hired by the college in 1930 as a

Albert W. Thompson Hall on the Washington State University campus in Pullman, which was completed in 1895, is the university's oldest building.

professor of Foreign Languages (his specialty was old French). In 1947 he became chair of the Division of Humanities and, in 1953, was named Dean of the College of Sciences and Art. He held that post until his retirement in 1964.

In 2000 Thompson Hall underwent another substantial interior renovation. The budget for the work was $7.6 million, which was more than 150 times the original cost of the building. In recent years, Thompson Hall—which remains one of the most iconic buildings on campus—has continued serving as the offices of the Dean of the College of Arts and Sciences, as well as providing classrooms and offices for the Department of Foreign Languages and Cultures.

48
St. Boniface Church, Convent and Rectory

46.5393° N, 117.0877° W

On St. Boniface Street in Uniontown

There's an almost fairytale quality to the St. Boniface Catholic Church, perched on a hill overlooking the small community of Uniontown. It's as if the church were too big and ornate for a town with a population of less than 400 people.

Uniontown traces its beginning to the arrival of Thomas Freeborn Montgomery in 1867. Montgomery had traveled west a few years earlier to escape the Civil War conflict, and in 1874 he filed a homestead claim on land that would become the site of Uniontown. Around the same time, large numbers of German and Swiss immigrants began settling throughout the Palouse, many either on or around Montgomery's holdings. In 1878 that population was large enough to support a post office. About a year later, Montgomery filed a town plat. The name Uniontown was chosen because the surrounding area was called Union Flats and the townsite was adjacent to Union Creek (apparently both of those names also were considered).

Many of the German settlers in Uniontown were devout Catholics originally from Bavaria, Baden, and Rhineland. They soon established a local parish, and in the brand-new town they built a small wooden church, which was enlarged three years later. By the mid-1880s, however, it had become apparent that the little wooden church was too small for the growing congregation. In 1888 the local pastor, Father Anton Joehren, began an effort to raise funds for a larger, more substantial church. Father Joehren, who has been described as a demanding and difficult man, was able to get construction started on the church foundations in 1893, but the work soon stopped, according to the city of Uniontown website, because of a dispute between him and some of the parishioners.

The following year, Father Joehren's temperament also caused the Benedictine Sisters, who had arrived in 1886 to teach in the local parochial school, to move their convent from Uniontown to nearby Colton (and, later, to Cottonwood, Idaho). In 1904, after Father Joehren was finally removed from his post, construction resumed on the church, which opened in April 1905 with a dedication ceremony. Five years later, in 1910, it was formally consecrated, making it the first Catholic Church in the state of Washington to earn that status.

The grand structure, which cost an estimated $20,000 (or nearly $715,000 in today's dollars) was built of Uniontown-made bricks on a locally quarried granite base. Designed in the Romanesque Revival style by a prominent Spokane architectural firm, Preusse and Zittel, the 57- by 140-foot church boasts striking twin spires that are about 145 feet tall, along with broad arches and corbelled brickwork and buttresses.

On either side of the church are a pair of matching brick buildings with granite foundations, which complement the church. The original rectory building, also completed in 1905, is a two-and-a-half-story structure with a white balcony. Though it was built to serve as a rectory, it was converted into a convent in 1912. The other structure, a similar-looking, two-story building completed in 1913, after the original rectory was made into a convent, became the new rectory and home of the parish priest.

Renamed St. Anthony's Convent, it served as the home of members of the Sisters of St. Francis order until the early 1930s. From 1932 to 1972, the convent housed the order of the Sisters of the Holy Names. Both orders served as teachers in the local parochial school. In the mid-1990s, the convent building was sold by the church and converted into a seven-room bed-and-breakfast known as the Churchyard Inn. That business, however, permanently closed during the COVID pandemic in 2020. At this writing, the property was for sale.

The St. Boniface Church complex, including the convent and rectory buildings, was added to the National Register of Historic Places in 1994. Sunday and Saturday masses and other services continue to be conducted in the church.

With its twin spires rising some 145 feet high, Uniontown's St. Boniface Catholic Church can be seen from miles around.

49

Whitman Mission National Historic Site

46.0414° N, 118.4640° W

On Whitman Mission Road, 13 Miles Southwest of Walla Walla

Despite the apparent peacefulness found today at the Whitman Mission National Historic Site, there is a tragic history associated with the place. Called *Waiilatpu* by the native Cayuse people (which translates as "The Place of the Rye Grass"), it was the site of a Presbyterian mission compound built by pioneer Dr. Marcus Whitman and other missionaries in 1842. It was there, in the winter of 1847, that Whitman, his wife Narcissa, and eleven other adult men were killed in what could best be described as a violent clash of cultures.

Dr. Whitman, who earned his medical degree from Fairfield Medical College in New York, had long wanted to be a missionary. With that goal in mind, in 1835, he traveled with another missionary, Samuel Parker, to what is now Montana and northern Idaho to minister to the indigenous Flathead and Nez Perce tribal nations.

After returning home, Dr. Whitman was eager to return west to continue his religious work. While in New York, he met and in 1836 married Narcissa Prentiss, a primary-school teacher whom Parker had introduced to him. Narcissa also desired to be a missionary. She came from a part of upstate New York known as the "Burned-Over District." It was a region that had seen so many intense Protestant religious revivals that the area was said to have been "set ablaze" by religious fervor.

Sponsored by the American Board of Commissioners for Foreign Missions, a group that promoted the development of Protestant missions throughout the undeveloped world, including the American West, the Whitmans joined with another missionary couple, Henry and Eliza Spaulding, in 1836 to travel overland to the Pacific Northwest, where they were tasked with establishing missions that would bring Christian teachings to the native people.

In making the eight-month journey on what would later be called the Oregon Trail, the two women became the first white women to cross the continental United States. Additionally, Narcissa made the trip while pregnant. The Whitmans' daughter, Alice Clarissa, born on March 14, 1837, after they arrived in the future state of Washington, was the first child born of U.S. citizens in the Pacific Northwest. Sadly, she would accidentally drown at age two.

The Spauldings decided to establish their mission among the Nez Perce people near present-day Lewiston, Idaho, while the Whitmans settled on Cayuse tribal land that was a bit farther west (near present-day Walla Walla). While the relationship between the Cayuse and the Whitmans was initially cordial, historians believe that over time frustrations began to build on both sides. The Cayuse had been promised payment for the use of their land and resources but never got it, while the Whitmans expected the native people to be eager to convert to Christianity as well as to take up farming and live like the whites (eschewing their traditional nomadic hunter-gatherer way of life).

Additionally, increasing numbers of white settlers began moving onto traditional Cayuse lands. The Whitman mission, in fact, became an important stop for those traveling on the Oregon Trail. These newcomers, unfortunately, also brought diseases, such as measles, against which the native population had no resistance.

When measles began to spread among the Cayuse, Dr. Whitman tried to help but could do little to save them. In addition, the native people saw that most of the newcomers survived the disease when they caught it (having a certain amount of natural immunity), while their people died in great numbers. Many of the Cayuse began to believe that Dr. Whitman was deliberately poisoning their brethren. Furthermore, in their culture, when a medicine man could not cure a patient, he was often slain for his failure. Either way, the missionaries were doomed.

On the morning of November 29, 1847, a group of Cayuse and others entered the mission compound and killed Whitman, his wife, and eleven others. They also took more than 40 of the other missionaries and their families as hostages. Eventually, the hostages were successfully ransomed by explorer Peter Skene Ogden, who was working on behalf of the Hudson's Bay Company.

In response to these events, political leaders in the Oregon Territory (which included Washington state at the time) raised an army of volunteers to fight in what became known as the Cayuse War. Following significant losses to this better-equipped force, in February 1850 members of the Cayuse, Nez Perce, and Walla Walla tribes agreed to give up the killers. They rounded up the five surviving members of the band that was believed to have attacked the mission and turned them over to federal military authorities, who had them hanged.

In 1897, on the 50th anniversary of the mission attack, two memorial structures were created near the former mission site: The Great Grave at the base of a hill overlooking the mission site, containing the remains of those who died (entombed beneath a massive slab of concrete engraved with their names) and the Whitman Memorial Shaft, a 27-foot-tall concrete obelisk erected at the top of the hill.

This 27-foot-tall concrete obelisk stands on a hill overlooking the former site of the Whitman Mission near Walla Walla. It was erected in 1897 to commemorate the site where Dr. Marcus Whitman, his wife, and eleven other missionaries were killed in 1847 following a tragic series of events.

As the years passed, the tragic story of the Whitman massacre, as it came to be known, evolved and grew. In 1936 the U.S. Congress created the Whitman National Monument (now the Whitman Mission National Historic Site) as a "public national memorial to Marcus Whitman and his wife, Narcissa Prentiss Whitman, who here established their Indian mission and school, and ministered to the physical and spiritual needs of the Indians until massacred with others in 1847."

To some, Whitman, his wife, and the other victims were martyrs to the conquest of the American West. When the state of Washington applied in 1953 to donate a statue to the National Statuary Hall in Washington D.C. (each state is afforded two such statues), it selected one of Marcus Whitman, who was (inaccurately) idealized as a muscular, rugged mountain man. The mission site was added to the National Register of Historic Places in 1966.

More recently, a number of historians have reexamined the narrative surrounding the Whitman killings and found the story is far more complicated than earlier accounts indicated. The event is no longer described as a "massacre," and the perspective of the native people has been given more attention. In 2021 Washington legislators voted to replace the Whitman statue with one honoring activist and humanitarian Billy Frank Jr., a Nisqually tribal member who was instrumental in securing and protecting tribal fishing rights on the Columbia River in the 20th century.

Today, the National Park Service oversees the site and operates a visitors' center that contains informative displays describing the mission and the tragic events that occurred there.

50
Liberty Theater

46.0403° N, 118.2010° W

On East Main Street in downtown Walla Walla

The three-story Liberty Theater on Main Street in downtown Walla Walla doesn't look like any other movie theater in Washington state. With its unusual Craftsman design, stained-glass windows, and glazed terra-cotta tile façade, the Liberty definitely doesn't resemble a typical multiplex.

Originally called the American Theater, the structure, built in 1917, was the creation of A. W. Eiler, who also operated the Bijou Grand Theater that was across the street (which Eiler closed when the American opened). According to historian Eric L. Flom, Eiler likely chose the theater's German-Dutch-influenced architecture because it was built at a time when many theaters incorporated faux Chinese, Egyptian, Arabian, and other exotic motifs.

Estimates are that the theater cost between $50,000 and $100,000 to build. Inside, it boasted marble tile with a balcony area carpeted in green velour. It could accommodate 1,000 people, who sat in seats made of mahogany and Spanish leather. The architects for the theater were the Walla Walla firm of Henry Osterman and Victor Siebert. Osterman had studied architecture in Germany while Siebert had started out as Osterman's apprentice before becoming a partner. The firm was also responsible for designing the Walla Walla Armory, the second Whitman County Courthouse, and a number of local schools.

In August 1917, the American opened with a showing of a Norma Talmadge silent film, *The Law of Compensation*. During the theater's first decade and a half, it hosted not only film presentations but live entertainment. In 1923 Eiler added a $25,000 Wurlitzer organ to the theater, which was placed in front of the screen, in the orchestra pit. The Wurlitzer was used until 1935, when the theater was refitted to accommodate the new "talkies." The organ was moved to a mortuary in Aberdeen, which in 1962 sold it for parts to several collectors.

In 1926 Eiler sold the American to a Yakima movie-house owner, Frederick Mercy, who changed the name of the theater to the Liberty. Mercy oversaw a major renovation of the theater's interior in 1939, designed by a Seattle architect named Bjarne Moe, who specialized in theater design. Moe's revisions incorporated the Moderne style of architecture that was popular in movie houses at the time. This included adding curving and streamlined walls with rounded corners and curving exit stairways. According to the building's National Register nomination, Moe also used lighting and lighting fixtures in such a way that the effect was "compelling the eye . . . of the patron to follow the path of design."

In 1980 the Liberty closed due to competition from the newer movie multiplexes that had opened in the city. About a decade later, the adjacent Bon Marche department store leased the theater building and incorporated it into its retail space. As part of the renovation, a false floor was placed on top of the theater's seats. The building was placed on the National Register of Historic Places in 1993.

The mid-2000s saw the Bon Marche's owner, Federated Department Stores, merge that company with its other store, Macy's, and in 2005, the theater space became part of Macy's.

The changes weren't over, however. In 2020 Macy's announced that it was closing its downtown Walla Walla location, including the former theater portion. The building was acquired by a local property-management company, which, in 2023, announced plans to restore and preserve it as a theater and special-events venue.

An interesting historical side note is the fact that the theater was built on the original site of Fort Walla Walla. The fort (and a second one later established on the same site) stood there from 1856 to the spring of 1858, when it relocated about three miles to the west. This third Fort Walla Walla, which operated until 1910, is now a museum and park and was added to the National Register of Historic Places in 1974.

Walla Walla's grand Liberty Theater, originally known as the American Theater, was constructed in 1917 to host silent movies (and later, "talkies") as well as live performances.

AFTERWORD

I think I would be remiss if I didn't spotlight two special places in Washington, not yet listed on the National Register, that are worthy of such recognition in the future. Both are architectural marvels that have become synonymous with the state.

The first, the Space Needle, is one of the most popular and most photographed landmarks in Seattle. Towering over the city at more than 600 feet high, this three-legged monolith is one of those structures that, upon seeing it, immediately tells a visitor that he or she is in the Emerald City.

The second, Grand Coulee Dam, is not only the largest producer of hydropower in the U.S., but is one of the biggest structures ever built by man. More massive than the Great Pyramid of Giza and using enough concrete to build a highway from Seattle to Miami, it is considered one of the seven Civil Engineering Wonders of the U.S. by the American Society of Civil Engineers.

51
The Space Needle

47.6205° N, 122.3493° W

On Broad Street in downtown Seattle

Few places are as closely associated with Washington state as Seattle's Space Needle tower. The 605-foot-tall spire has been described as a modern engineering marvel. When it was completed in 1962, it was not only the tallest building in Seattle, but the tallest structure west of the Mississippi River (it has since lost that designation to the 1,215-foot-high Kennecott Garfield Smelter Stack near Magna, Utah).

The Needle, which is not yet listed on the National Register of Historic Places but was designated an official Seattle landmark in 1999, served as the centerpiece for the Century 21 Exposition (commonly known as the 1962 Seattle's World's Fair).

Like many complex construction projects, the Needle was the result of the efforts of several individuals. The basic idea for the tower was conceived by Seattle businessman Edward E. Carlson, who, after dining at a restaurant atop a broadcast tower in Stuttgart, Germany, in 1959, thought the upcoming World's Fair event in Seattle needed a similar restaurant in the sky. Carlson sketched his idea on several postcards, which he mailed to fair officials, including James Douglas, vice president of fair construction. Douglas suggested to Carlson that he reach out to an architect, John Graham Jr., who had recently completed the design and construction of a revolving restaurant in Hawaii.

Graham jumped at the opportunity and enlisted a team of his associates, including Victor Steinbrueck and John Ridley. The group considered several concepts, including a structure that resembled a tethered balloon and a spire topped by some sort of flying saucer (a version of which was ultimately selected). Steinbrueck also had the idea for the wasp-waisted tripod for the building's "legs," while Ridley came up with a way to build a double-deck crown atop the structure. The concept was to reflect the fair's space-age, futuristic theme.

After failing to obtain public funding for the project, Graham joined with four other Pacific Northwest business leaders, Bagley Wright, Ned Skinner, Norton Clapp, and Howard S. Wright, to form a private company, which they called the Pentagram Corporation, to finance and build the project. Howard Wright's construction company, which his family had operated in Seattle since 1929, served as the building contractor and Edward Carlson, who was vice president of Western Hotels, agreed to run the facility, which now included a revolving restaurant on the top of the structure.

The group purchased from the city of Seattle an obsolete fire department alarm center in the Queen Anne neighborhood for the location of the new Space Needle project. Construction of the project proved a model of efficiency. Work began on April 17, 1961, with the laying of the foundation (the largest continuous concrete pour ever attempted on the west coast at that time—5,850 tons in just over 12 hours). Within a short time, the steel tower began to rise above the city on legs anchored by 74 bolts, each 32 feet long. On December 8, 1961, workers topped off the structure, and the restaurant hosted a special gala on March 24, 1962, less than a month before the fair was to open. In the end, the massive project, which cost $4.5 million, was completed in only 400 days.

To ensure the Needle's stability, the structure, which weighs 8,660 metric tons, was built to withstand winds of more than 200 miles per hour and to handle earthquakes of magnitudes up to 9.1.

During the fair, 2.65 million people visited the Space Needle, making it one of the fair's most popular attractions. Most ascended aboard one of the tower's three elevators, although the tower could be climbed via its 848 stairs. Also during the fair, the spire was topped with a natural-gas torch that lit up at night with rainbow colors (the torch was removed after the fair ended).

Over the years, the Needle has been updated and modified. In 1982 the Skyline level (which was in the original plans) was added at the 100-foot mark, which included another restaurant. The structure was upgraded and renovated in 2000 and again in 2017–18.

Built in 1962 for the Seattle World's Fair, the giant Space Needle is one of the city's most recognizable structures.

52
Grand Coulee Dam

47.9566° N, 118.9810° W

On WA State Route 155 North, 4 miles from Grand Coulee

Another iconic structure not yet on the National Register of Historic Places is Grand Coulee Dam, in the north-central part of Washington. The statistics related to the dam are impressive: it cost $300 million (or more than $7 billion in today's dollars); it is one of the largest concrete structures in the world (and the largest in the U.S.); it was built using more than 12 million cubic feet of concrete; and it is the largest single producer of electricity in the country.

At 5,223 feet wide—just 57 feet short of a mile— Grand Coulee is four times the width of Nevada's famous Hoover Dam. Its hydro-powered generators produce more than 21 billion kilowatt hours of electricity annually, which is enough to power more than 2 million households with electricity for a year.

Not surprisingly, the story of how such a massive dam came to be built in a remote section of Washington is a complex one. The first talk about building a major dam surfaced in about 1918, when Wenatchee newspaper publisher Rufus Woods began advocating in his paper for a dam to provide water to the Columbia Plateau lands. Joined by two Ephrata attorneys, Billy Clapp and James O'Sullivan, who were equally enthusiastic supporters of such a project, the trio promoted the economic benefits of a Columbia basin dam.

O'Sullivan is credited with suggesting that since nature had once regularly blocked the Columbia basin with ice dams that forced water onto the dry Grand Coulee riverbed area (during the so-called Missoula Floods of the Ice Age, which occurred more than 20,000 years ago), a high, manmade dam could accomplish the same result and produce plenty of hydroelectric power for the western states.

In 1932 newly elected president Franklin D. Roosevelt agreed to support the construction of a dam in the Grand Coulee area, but was concerned about the cost and only agreed to fund a lower dam (one about 150 feet tall from the bedrock) than supporters wanted (which was 550 feet). Roosevelt, however, agreed it should be built with a foundation that could support a higher dam in the future.

Work began on the shorter dam in 1933. Then, in August 1934, Roosevelt visited the construction site and decided to support funding for the higher dam, which was approved by Congress in 1935. The main reason for the change of heart was that the president saw how a larger dam project would fit into his political goals of establishing large-scale public jobs programs to help lift the country out of the Great Depression.

The enormous project, completed in 1942, employed more than 11,000 men, who worked more than 27 million hours diverting the Columbia River during construction, digging the foundations, and pouring the concrete. The water-powered turbines and generators installed at the dam were, at the time, the largest ever built.

While there was initially some skepticism that sparsely populated western states would need the amount of electricity produced by the dam's two power plants, that idea was quickly put to rest with the advent of World War II. Within months of becoming operational, the dam began to send electricity to wartime factories that built airplanes (in Seattle) and ships (in Vancouver, Washington, and Portland, Oregon). At the conclusion of the war, the dam's irrigation pumps were installed and it began providing water to some 670,000 acres of land in

Considered one of the engineering marvels of the world, Grand Coulee Dam is the largest concrete structure in the U.S. and the single largest producer of electricity in the country. Completed in 1942, it would certainly be an appropriate future addition to the National Register of Historic Places.

the Columbia Basin. In 1974 the dam's electrical capacity was increased with the addition of a third power plant.

Despite all the superlatives surrounding the project (it was described as the "Eighth Wonder of the World" when it was completed), over the years it has been the subject of some controversy. Its construction required the displacement of between 3,000 and 4,000 people, many of whom lived on small farms and in small communities in the Grand Coulee area. Additionally, as part of the larger Columbia Basin Project, which includes four other dams, three storage lakes, and some 2,300 miles of irrigation canals, it eliminated wild salmon runs on the upper Columbia River, which had played a key role in the diet and culture of the region's Native American population. The late historian Cassandra Tate noted that the social and environmental costs of the dam were such that, according to a 2000 study, it "probably could not be built today."

SELECTED BIBLIOGRAPHY

Note: This book relied heavily on the documentation included on the National Register of Historic Places nomination forms. That documentation can be found at: https://www.nps.gov/subjects/nationalregister/database-research.htm

I also consulted multiple articles originally published in www.HistoryLink.org, the free online encyclopedia of the history of the Washington state, as well as multiple articles in: the *Adams County News*, the *Associated Press*, the *Chehalis Daily Chronicle*, the *Ellensburg Daily Record*, the *Los Angeles Times*, the *Seattle Times*, the *Spokane Spokesman-Review*, the *Tri-Cities Area Journal of Business*, the *Walla Walla News-Bulletin,* and the *Yakima Herald.*

Artifacts Consulting, Inc. June 2003. *Washington State Historic County Courthouse Assessment,* prepared for the Washington State Office of Archaeology and Historic Preservation, Olympia, WA

Atomic Heritage Foundation. 2011. *B Reactor: The First in the World*, prepared for the U.S. Department of Energy's Richland Operations Office, Washington DC

Elliott, T. C. October 1927. *Steptoe Butte and Steptoe Battlefield.* The Washington Historical Quarterly, Vol. 18, No. 4, published by the University of Washington, Seattle

Engstrom, Wesley C. 2007. *Spirit of Liberty: History of a Gold Mining Camp and Its School*, Self-published, Cle Elem, WA

Engstrom, Wesley C. 2006. *Swauk Basin History: Gold Created a Community*, prepared as part of the Swauk Basin Wildlife Protection Plan, Cle Elem, WA

Gulick, Bill. 1996. *Traveler's History of Washington*, Caxton Press, Caldwell, ID

Hayes, Katie. August 23, 2018. "Daylight Properties Purchases Three Historic Chehalis Buildings, Opens Office," *The Daily Chronicle*, Chehalis, WA

Johnston, Mike. March 28, 2015. "Living History in Liberty," *Ellensburg Daily Record*, Ellensburg, WA

Lambeth, Robert M. Accessed August 4, 2024. "St. Boniface Church in Uniontown," Spokane Historical, https://spokanehistorical.org/items/show/425

Langford, Theresa. 2011. *Exploring Fort Vancouver,* University of Washington Press, Seattle

McIntyre, Hannah. April 23, 2023. "Early Stages of Restoration Begin for Historic Liberty Theater in Downtown Walla Walla," *Walla Walla Union-Bulletin*, Walla Walla, WA

Mittendorf, Robert. July 22, 2023. "Iconic Bellingham Building is Getting a Face-lift. Here's How You Can Watch the Progress," *Bellingham Herald*, Bellingham, WA

Reed, Conner. August 2020. "The Bizarre History of the Maryhill Museum of Art," *Portland Magazine* vol. 16, issue 6. Portland, OR

Scott, Lea Anne. Accessed March 28, 2023. "The Steptoe Defeat, 1858," Spokane Historical, https://spokanehistorical.org/items/show/235

Sorensen, Eric, April 2014. "Lost Highway," *Washington State Magazine*, vol. 13, no. 3. Pullman, WA

Speidel, William C. 1967. *Sons of the Profits or There's No Business Like Grow Business: The Seattle Story 1851-1901*, Nettle Creek Publishing Co., Seattle

Strong, William Duncan, and Schenck, W. Egbert. January-March 1925. "Petroglyphs near The Dalles of the Columbia River," *American Anthropologist,* vol. 27, no. 1. American Anthropological Association, Washington DC

Tate, Cassandra. 2020. *Unsettled Ground: The Whitman Massacre and Its Shifting Legacy in the American West*, Sasquatch Books, Seattle

Thompson, Erwin N. 1964. "Whitman Mission National Historic Site," National Park Service Historical Handbook Series No. 37, Washington, DC

Tuhy, John. 1983. *Sam Hill: The Prince of Castle Nowhere*, Timber Press, Portland, OR

INDEX

Richard Moreno is the author of 15 books, including *Frontier Fake News: Nevada's Sagebrush Humorists and Hoaxsters* and *Roadside History of Nevada*. He graduated from the University of California, Davis with a bachelor's degree in Political Science and, later, earned a master's degree in Journalism at Columbia University in New York. He is a lecturer in the Department of Communication at Central Washington University and a regular contributor to *1883 Magazine* in Kittitas County. He lives in Ellensburg with his wife and cat.